The author was born in July 1923 and attended the then Kingsbury Grammar School. Joining the RAF in 1942, he became a Flight Engineer and flew on operations from July 1944 until the war ended.

He trained as a Patent Agent and following retirement, wrote this collection initially for his family.

Dedication

To my family and my friends Milly, Paul and Zena who have encouraged me in this eccentric exercise.

Harold Kirby

FROM BARD TO VERSE

A Miscellany of Rhymes
and Other Items

AUSTIN MACAULEY PUBLISHERS™

LONDON • CAMBRIDGE • NEW YORK • SHARJAH

A CIP catalogue record for this title is available from the British Library.

ISBN 9781787102453 (Paperback)
ISBN 9781787102460 (E-Book)

www.austinmacauley.com

First Published (2018)
Austin Macauley Publishers Ltd.
25 Canada Square
Canary Wharf
London
E14 5LQ

Acknowledgements

My thanks go to the members of my family and friends who have encouraged me in producing various rhymes and other items over several years and suggested I collect them together in a book. Also, my thanks go to members of my publishers, Austin Macauley, who have helped to bring this into fruition.

Introduction

It really started in 1986 when a friend, Richard, was President of our Rotary Club. Richard, at that time, had a Gents' Outfitters and Dress Hire Shop, and was an ardent member of The Richard III Society which, at that time, held that King Richard was not as bad as had been portrayed by the succeeding Tudors, was not a hunchback and was not responsible for killing the Princes in the Tower. Be that as it may, the modern Richard was quite a character in himself, and at his President's Evening, I read a humorous 'tribute' in rhyme which, in view of his connection with Richard III, I wrote in the form of Shakespeare, the Bard of Avon, and called it Richard IV. Sometime after that, I started to write mainly humorous rhymes and other items for my own and my family's and friends' amusement which I have collected together. Hence the title of this collection.

Some of my early items were inspired by verses from a book of poems by A. A. Milne entitled *When We Were Very Young*, and these early items, together with others, appear in the opening section of the collection which I have called 'Now We Are Not So Young'.

Contents

Section I

Now We Are Not So Young

Halfway Up (or Down)

Halfway up the stairs is a stair where I stop,
For it's quite a long way from the bottom to top.
Then after I've rested I think with a frown
Was I on my way up, or was I going down?

Lost

Where was it I put them I'd just like to know.
I'm sure that I had them a short while ago.
They're not on the landing, they're not in the hall;
(They were when I made my last telephone call).
In guest room and study I've just drawn a blank,
And they're certainly not on the hot water tank.
They're not on the worktop nor under the sink,
(Though how they'd have got there I just cannot think).
The microwave's empty, the cupboard is bare,
And they're not down the sides of my fav'rite armchair.
They're not in the wardrobe nor under the bed,
And not in the greenhouse or even the shed.
I've looked everywhere, and it's just as I feared,
They're nowhere at all, and they've just disappeared.
Why are you grinning? I don't think it's kind
To laugh at a person who's trying to find
Their specs which are missing. What is it you said?
They're not lost but just pushed to the top of my head.

Mislaid

I came to Tesco's not two hours ago,
And now I cannot remember the row,
Where I parked my car. I've looked all around
But I've no idea where it may be found.
I'm perfectly sure it cannot be far.
Has anyone seen my car?

The body is coloured metallic blue,
And the grille is chrome and the wheel trims too.
There's a dent or two in the nearside wing
And the boot is secured by a length of string.
I can't find my car though I've looked everywhere,
And nobody seems to care.

I'm told my memory is rather poor,
Though I've never mislaid my car before.
I know you'll think I'm a terrible pain,
But a sudden thought has come into my brain.
I'm really sorry I made such a fuss,
I recall, now, I came in the Tesco bus!

The Name

What will they call the young couple's offspring?
Will it be Cruz, Beck, Genoa, Brooklyn?
I know they've considered a host of names
From Alix to Zig (no Thomas or James).
Whatever it is I'm willing to bet
That when he gets older it's one he'll regret.
We must be thankful it wasn't a craze
To choose such odd names in our parent's days.

Now there's a surprise; they've settled on Jim.
But I've made a mistake; it's a 'her', not a 'him'!

Autumn Afternoon

Where am I going? I wish I knew
Just what it was I wanted to do.
Doctor or dentist, bank or bazaar?
Wherever it is, it cannot be far.

As I rack my brain the cold winds blow
The clouds above and the leaves below,
And while I walk I try to recall,
Why it is I am here at all.

Across the green and round by the square,
Through the arcade and past 'The Black Bear',
Cafe or chemist or bakery;
I have no idea where I want to be.

Up through the high street, back through the town,
Past the old cinema, now closed down.
I don't want the florist, I am sure,
And I take the bus to the superstore.

It isn't bingo, I'm sure of that,
Because I always go there with Pat.
I've passed the station, bus stop too,
So where I am off to I haven't a clue.

Over the bridge and past the Town Hall,
Then through the park by the swimming pool.
I'm sure if I saw it I would know
Just where it was I wanted to go.

I am afraid that my memory is not as good as it used to be.
But I've just remembered! Silly me!
I'm on my way home from the old folks' tea!

Growing Older (But not Wiser)

I won a packet at Chepstow races;
Four outright wins and two each-way places.
It's my first time alone at steeplechases.
Who'll celebrate with me?

A nice young man who I met over tea
Said he would look after my winnings for me.
"For muggers will target lone women," said he.
Who'll celebrate with me?

He kindly came to the station with me
And asked me to wait while he went for a pee.
He hasn't come back, and now I can see
Who'll celebrate? Not me!

I won a packet at Chepstow races;
And now it's all gone without any traces.
I'm glad you can't see how red my face is.
How could I be so silly?

The Grandsons

I've football-mad grandsons; they're called Lou and Fred.
Lou supports Chelsea in blue; Fred favours Arsenal in red.
They argue all day who's the best of the two,
If it's Arsenal in red or it's Chelsea in blue.

When I go to matches with my grandson Lou
I must always remember to wear my scarf (blue),
But if I'm with Fred I must put on instead
A different garment like my beret (red).

I love my two grandsons really I do
Both Frederick (red) and Ludovic (blue).
So there are some days in the year that I dread;
And when Arsenal play Chelsea I take to my bed.

Angeline

Angeline wrote words obscene
Upon a wall in Palmers Green
Then hurried off, but she was seen;
The fuzz went after her 'Angeline!'

"Angeline, what did they mean?"
The Magistrate asked as she stood between
Two men in blue in Palmers Green.
"Those words you wrote. What do they mean?"

"Angeline, I see you've been deprived as a child in Palmers
Green,
And placed in care when just thirteen,
So I'll let you off with your record clean."

Angeline, with record clean,
And very quickly off the scene,
Wrote further words in Palmers Green.
"The beak's a *****" wrote Angeline.

Memories

"I'd like to go," the old man said, and rubbed a tear-filled eye.
"To where I met my own dear love in far-off days gone by.
I'd like to see the village hall where I first held her hand
As we sat through some foreign film we couldn't understand.
I want to wander through the woods and see that shady dell
Where Bess and I first shyly kissed, beguiled by Cupid's spell.
I'd like to walk beside the stream to that secluded place
Beneath the bridge where oft we stayed entwined in close embrace,
And see the seat where Bess and I sat talking, ardour fanned,
About our youthful hopes and fears, our lives together planned."
The old man then fell silent and he gave a drawn-out sigh;
Still dreaming of the times long passed, he wiped his other eye.
"He's wandering," his daughter said. "Do you suppose he's ill?"
"I'm sure he is," his son replied, "as mother's name was Jill."

Paradise Lost

I always dreamed that, when retired, we'd live down by the sea.
It soon became, when I stopped work, a grand reality.

We bought a little cottage in a village near a bay,
And we were very happy there, and could be still today.

The village store was yards away; a bus-stop just outside.
We used the bus to go to town; a very pleasant ride.

We quickly joined the village life, the Church and Social Club,
And made some further friendships at the quiz-nights in the pub.

When sitting in the garden we can watch the ships sail past.
We thought we'd found the perfect place but idylls cannot last.

The village store was first to go; they found it would not pay
When supermarkets in the town took their best trade away.

The local school has now been closed on grounds of costs they say.
The children now are being bussed to one six miles away.

And now we get one bus a day but passengers are few.
It gets to town at one o'clock and leaves again at two.

A lot of locals have now moved to find some work elsewhere.
The Social Club's lost members and disbandment's in the air.

The brewers have now sold the pub as custom had declined.

In place of it six blocks of flats are to be built we find.

And now we've heard the Post Office is shortly to close down,
And then the nearest one will be four miles away in town.

The Newsagent has told me that he certainly can't stay
If powers that be take his Post Office business away.

My wife and I would like to move, though once life here was
bliss,
But who on earth would buy our house with few amenities!

Customer Service

I wanted to query my last account
As it seemed to include a wrong amount.
Now a telephone call without a doubt
I was sure would rapidly sort it out.
A recorder answered the call of mine.
"Welcome," it said "to our Customer Line.
We'll deal with your problem efficiently
If you follow these options carefully.
If a product is faulty, please press ONE."
(At least my enquiry has now begun)
"For electrical products, please press TWO."
(Oh do hurry up; I want to get through)
"If your goods are still under guarantee,
We would be obliged if you now press THREE. Though if
you've had the same problem before,
We suggest that you now press button FOUR.
If your ordered product failed to arrive,
You'll get our carriers on button FIVE.
If you've self-assembly goods you can't fix,
You'll find help at hand if you press SIX,
And SEVEN's the button you should press
If you wish to exchange a coat or dress.
In order to change a delivery date
We suggest that you now press button EIGHT,
And NINE is the button you should select
If the goods we sent you are incorrect.
In order to hear these options again
You'll hear them once more if you press TEN.
If you have a problem not optioned here
We've trained staff to help you, never fear,
So if you'd like someone to speak to you,
Continue to hold and we'll put you through.

All our agents are busy we regret,
So we cannot connect you to one just yet,
But rest assured you've been put in a queue,
And while you wait here's some music for you.
And if you find you really can't wait,
Please ring us again at some later date.
We value your custom so don't forget,
You can now order goods by internet."

I can't hang on longer; it's too wearying,
And this call's now cost more than the sum I was querying.

The Visit

"Please do come in; take off your hat;
I'm looking forward to our chat;
It's really nice of you to call;
I rarely see someone at all.
I don't get out as much as I
Was able to in days gone by,
As with my legs so bad I've found
I miss what's going on around.
You know Miss Smith upon the hill;
It seems that she is very ill.
It's something that she ate, they say.
You can't tell what's in food today.
And Mrs Brown at twenty-two
Is really feeling rather blue
Because they will not operate,
Until she loses much more weight.

At number sixteen Mrs Cash
Has come out in a nasty rash.
Some people blame the strawberries,
Though others say it's caused by fleas.
Old Mr Smith at number three
Was climbing in an apple tree
And, reaching for an apple, fell
And broke an arm and leg as well.
And opposite, at number four
Miss Harper's health is rather poor.
I really shouldn't tell you this;
It's rumoured she smokes cannabis.
And Mr Johnson down the lane
Is laid up with his back again.
The fitness course that he'd begun

29

They said was clearly overdone.

Poor Mr Squires at number eight
His liver's in a dreadful state.
I'm sure he has too much to drink.
At least that's what his neighbours think.
His wife must find it such a strain.
I'm sure it causes her migraine.
If that's the case it's very sad,
Though some say she is just as bad.
And Mrs Green at number five
Is lucky to be still alive.
Her daily pills she quite forgot,
And Saturday she took the lot.
What would have happened, goodness knows
If she had not had placebos.
And Mrs Gray across the street
Is having trouble with her feet.
Her gout is very bad I hear.
Oh must you go so soon my dear?
I'm sorry that you have to go.
I have enjoyed our chat you know.
Do come again; I've more to tell
Of neighbours that are not so well.
Though, as I said, I'm out of touch,
And cannot tell you very much."

The Last Straw

Oh, Doris I've had such a morning. My head's in a terrible spin.
They've started to dig up the road, dear, and making a deafening d i n .

The newsagent left the wrong paper, and Roger went off in a huff;
He was saving coupons for air miles, and now he will not have enough.

The toaster gave us a burnt offering, the fuse on the kettle has blown,
The kitchen sink's outlet is blocked, and the plumber won't answer the phone.

The washing machine's started leaking; there's water all over the floor,
And Lassie's had pups in the hallway, and no-one can use the front door.

The line with the washing has broken, and dropped all the clothes in the mud,
And I pricked my finger when sewing
So my needlepoint's spotted with blood.

The seal on the freezer has perished, and we've week-end guests due to stay;
The joint that I was to give them will have to be eaten today.

I'm sorry I'll have to ring off now; I see it's a quarter past three.
I've forgotten to buy any muffins, and the Vicar is coming to tea.

Freedom

It's our first time away without children along,
And although we are free it somehow seems wrong.
I can't play beach cricket, search rock pools alone.
What am I to do dear, now we're on our own?
I can't build sandcastles or splash in the sea.
With no children around, there's just you and me.
I cannot recall, though I've thought hard and long,
What we did long ago before kids came along.

Sats

This was written at the time when there were some educationists who disputed whether
The results of the Scholastic Assessment Tests (SATs)
Gave an accurate assessment of a child's educational grade.

Deer Unkeljack I told you that I took my sats in may
I wated months for my results they came at larst today.
IfI shoud parse my english sat yore hat you sed youd eat.
Pleese tell me me wen you do it as Id luv to see thatfeet. They
sed my spelings rarther week and reedings not so good and of
the set books and the plaise I new less than I shoud.
Butfelt that in the coarse of time these problems coud be beet,
And gav me a top graid because my righting was so neet.

The Christmas Present

At Christmas last my children came to bring their gift to me.
They said, "We think you'll love it," so I couldn't wait to see.
I took the wrapping off and found they'd bought me a Satnav.
They told me they considered it was something I should have.
It would, they said, locate for me some unfamiliar places
And thus enable me to see a number of new faces.
It would, moreover, guide me on a route from door to door,
And stop me getting lost in towns I'd not been to before;
And it would also find at once the best and quickest way
To my resort when I decide to go on holiday.
But as it was then far too cold to do much travelling,
I put it carefully away to use it in the spring.
And then I thought I'd get it out to find my way around,
But where I'd *put* it I forget and now it can't be found.
So when it's Christmas time again, there's something I must have;
An instrument to help locate my still unused Satnav!

The Satnav

I started off quite early one sunny day in May
With my new Satnav in the car to guide me on my way.
It led me down some leafy lanes through hamlets by the score,
Past many pretty villages that I'd not seen before.
The Satnav gave directions where no signpost was in sight,
Though s o m e t i m e s told me to turn left
When I thought it should be right.
I lunched outside a country inn beside a village green,
And watched swans preening on a pond, a quite idyllic scene.
I passed by many beauty spots by routes before untried,
And thoroughly enjoyed what was a very pleasant ride.
At last I reached my journey's end; I thought a perfect day,
But when I got out of my car I found to my dismay
My final destination was not the one I'd meant;
I'd gone to Gillingham, Dorset, and not to Gillingham, Kent.

The Job

I found the shed doors sticking after months of winter rain.
To solve the problem I should need to go and get my plane.
It wasn't in the garage and it wasn't in the shed,
So guessed it was with other tools I kept indoors instead.
But on the way I noticed on a nearby patch of ground;
A sapling, really more a tree, with tangled shrubs around.
I didn't want the sapling there, so went to get my saw
To cut it quickly down before it grew some more.
But having got the saw I found to my dismay,
I couldn't cut the tree down 'til the shrubs were cleared away.
So then I got my secateurs to make room for the saw,
But as the shrubs were very thick this task became a chore.
Eventually the job was done and I cut down the tree,
Which left me with another task of clearing the debris.
This took some time as there was quite a lot about,
And by the time I finished, my inside was crying out.
No wonder I was hungry as my watch said ten to two.
By then I'd clean forgotten what I first set out to do.

Bogey

To her husband one day his wife said, "Ben,
If I go first will you marry again?"
Intent on a book with a drink close by,
"I might," he murmured to her in reply.
"And would you let her live in our house here?"
He murmured again, "Well, I might, my dear."
"And allow her to drive my Triumph Sprite?"
Once more he said to his wife, "I might."
"And let her sit in my own armchair,
And use my new dryer to dry her hair,
And possibly sleep in my own dear bed?"
Again to her questions "I might," he said.
"And use my own golf clubs? Please be candid."
"Oh no," he said. "The girl's left-handed."

The Ceiling

My ceiling was quite bad after years of some neglect
So I decided that I'd make it my next big project.
I cleared the working surfaces, the window sills as well
And put some plastic sheeting down to catch the drips that fell.
Then went to buy emulsion paint from our self-service store,
And as my brushes were quite old I went to get some more.

When I got home I went to get my old step-ladder in
And opened the emulsion paint, all eager to begin.
So up the ladder then I went with paint pot and with brush.
To get the painting quickly done I started with a rush.
Upon the ceiling I spread paint here, there and everywhere,
Though some ran down my painting arm and some fell in my
hair.

Eventually the job was done, though took more than a day.
At last I could put ladder, brushes and the paint away.
I'm not an expert, but I thought the end result not bad,
Although in parts maybe another coating could have had.
When in a local shop next day a neighbour I did see,
And said, "It's some time since we met." and asked her in to
tea.

She helped me with the washing up, and as she dried a cup
I saw her looking round about, and then start looking up.
She said "Your ceiling's getting bad. It's time you had it done,
And if you'd like a workman in I know the very one."

The Shed

As the weather was warm and the forecast fine,
I decided to clear out the old shed of mine.
So I took out the mower, the pruner and shears,
And a number of tools that I'd not seen for years,
Some old tins of paint that had then turned quite hard, and a
bucket that leaked, and a rusty fireguard.
I found a few baskets that once held some fruit,
And a mouse's nest in a Wellington boot;
Some jars full of liquid without a label,
And a twenty-foot coil of electric cable,
Two old tennis racquets with some broken strings
And a clockwork alarm clock that no longer rings,
Some off-cuts of carpets of emerald green,
And several sheets of clear polythene,
Odd shoes and a hammer whose head had worked loose,
Some boxes of items that might come in use,
And lastly two deck-chairs with canvases torn,
Which I stacked with the rest outside on the lawn.
I threw out the things that I wanted no more,
And then took a broom and swept the shed floor.
And after I'd done that I went straight ahead
And put the rest of the things back in the shed.
But one thing that puzzles me still to this day;
Despite all the items that I threw away,
I still cannot fathom why after I'd done
There's less room in the shed than when I'd begun!

Election Fever

Election Day's coming and I'm at a loss
As I've no idea where I should put a cross.
For candidate A has some views I don't share,
And B's from a party I really can't bear;
C's a big gas-bag but says nothing new,
And some of D's statements I can't think are true;
E's views of the future I cannot believe,
And F's full of promises he can't achieve.
Their differing forecasts I find just confuse,
Which makes it a problem which one I should choose.
So I'll vote for one who I know cannot win
Then I cannot be blamed for which party gets in.

My Age

"Do you feel your age?" the young man asked.
"You're ninety now, I'm told.
I can't imagine how I'd feel if I became that old."
"But do I feel my age you asked. I can't say that I do.
I'm not as agile as I was, and that is clearly true.
But I am not too bad apart from my arthritic knees,
And when I'm walking up a hill I am inclined to wheeze.
And if I'm sitting down too long I find it hard to stand,
And getting on and off a bus I need a helping hand.
Sometimes I find it hard to hear, especially in a crowd
So conversation's difficult with background noise so loud.
These days I find I must take care about the things I eat,
And favourite foods I must decline because they now repeat.
And simple jobs take longer than they used to, that I know,
And I must rest more frequently than I did years ago.
My memory problems cause me to forget things now and then.
So no, I don't feel ninety. More like a hundred and ten!"

The Lesson

The teacher stood before the boys,
And raised his hand to quell the noise
"Now pay attention, boys," said he
"And I will show a DVD
As we have got a new projector
Suggested by the Schools Inspector.
Just wait a minute while I look
Into this short instruction book,
And in a moment we shall see
How science has changed through history."
So through the book he quickly scanned,
But found it hard to understand.

The terms it used to him were new
And bluntly he had not a clue.
"Be patient for a while," said he
"I'll have it working presently.
If that goes there and this goes here
Words on the screen should soon appear."
But though he tried with might and main
All of his efforts were in vain.
"It must be faulty," he explained,
As still the screen quite blank remained.
The lesson wasn't quite as planned
And then the worst boy raised his hand.
"What is it boy?" the master said,
His face by this time very red,
"And if you think this is a lark
And make some infantile remark,
I'll send you straightway to the head."
"Sir, not at all," the young boy said.
"I was about to ask if you

Would let me see what I could do."
"Think you'll do better? Come and try"
Was the Form Master's quick reply,
As failure by the boy would do
To take him down a peg or two.
But the young student took a look,
Ignoring the instruction book.
Apparently he had no need,
As fingers moved at lightning speed,
And suddenly the class all cheered,
As on the screen some words appeared.
"History of Science" all could see
To introduce the DVD.

The master watched it in surprise.
He just could not believe his eyes,
And wondered how it came to be
An eight-year-old knew more than he.
Then gave a deep despairing sigh
At what had clearly passed him by
For scientific education
Seemed to have skipped a generation.

Section II

The Farmer's Year

Springtime

Oh, to be in England now that April's there?
Where the frost has caught the blossom and laid the orchard bare.
Where the cows have got mastitis and the hens refuse to lay,
And the cost of feed has risen, and there's income tax to pay.
Where the fields are under water and the tractor's up the creek,
And the pigs refuse to fatten, and the rent was due last week.
I hope you're not downhearted, but it is my firm belief you'd
be better off in Palma or with me in Tenerife.

Summer

When summer droughts have left their mark, and banks are threatening to foreclose,
Just make your fields a pleasure park and claim a bounty of Euros.

Autumn

(It was written when the UK was a member of EU, formerly EEC)

We plough the fields and scatter the good seed on the land,
But Brussels regulations are hard to understand.

They sell us fertiliser to help to swell the grain,
But as we've sold our quota, we must plough it back again.
Directions by the thousand the EU sends to me,
But thank them all, yes thank them all for ev'ry subsidy.

Winter

When winter comes don't think you can relax.
It's time to seek a further loan to pay the income tax,
And buy some further cattle feed as stocks are getting low,
And stop the barn roof caving in beneath the weight of snow.
However seasons do not last, and fortunes can reverse,
So next year may be better, though I fear it could be worse.

On Teaching a Relative to Drive

The steering wheel's before your seat.
Below the pedals for your feet.
Clutch left, accelerator right,
What did you say? Your belt's too tight?
Well loosen it. I'll start once more.
That central pedal on the floor
Is for the brakes both front and rear.
The gear selector lever's here.
Four forward gears, reverse just one.
No, don't despair I've nearly done.
There is some more, but not that much.
That pedal there is for the clutch.
The handbrake is this lever here
To use when parking. Yes my dear,
It does seem quite a lot to know,
But try to learn before we go
As High Street drivers have strong views
On motorists who while they choose
Which pedal is for changing gear
Hold up the traffic at the rear.
Before you start the engine just
Remember that this lever must
In neutral be or you could shunt
Into the car that's just in front.
And don't forget, if you are wise,
That feet and hand must synchronise
Their movements when you change your gear
Or dreadful noises you will hear
Beneath the car, but don't despair,
They tell you that the gear's still there.

All ready then? Away we go.
No! Gently! There you've stalled. No
I wasn't shouting. Try once more.
Your foot lift slowly from the floor.
You've got it moving. Good. Now see
That turning on the left. Dear me!
I meant the road that's just ahead.
We're in our neighbour's drive instead.

We cannot turn. You'll have to back.
I'm sure that you'll soon get the knack.
Oh dear! You should have looked behind
Before reversing, never mind,
I'm sure our neighbour won't be cross,
That cat of his is no great loss.
But not so quickly through the gate
I say! That woman's in a state.
Her standing jump was quite immense.
She nearly cleared the garden fence.
Swing the car round now we're out.
Ignore that rude pedestrian's shout,
And settle down; engage first gear,
And pull out – WHEN the road is clear.
Signalling left when turning right
Gave that truck driver quite a fright.
He seems more than a trifle fraught,
But even so he didn't ought
To use such language. Just ignore
Him, though I see what's made him sore.
When braking he upset his load,
And now it's blocking half the road.
Our way is clear, so pull away.
I do not think it wise to stay.
Go right at the next round-about.
No dear. I didn't mean to shout.
I was just taken by surprise.
It's usual to go round clockwise.

But never mind. I'm sure you'll learn,
Though now I think we should return.

Slow down a bit; it's not a race.
You should not go at such a pace
Through traffic lights when they are red
With policemen in the road ahead.
You really made that policeman hop.
I think he wanted you to stop.
We've done enough today, I think.
I feel that I have earned a drink.
Another lesson? I can't say.
My diary's full for many a day.
You'll have to wait a while I fear.
I've no free time until next year.

The Telephone

Sometimes when the phone rings I know that it will stop
For it is on the ground floor and I sleep at the top.
So I dial 1471 to see whose calling me,
In case it is a friend in need who wants me urgently,
And irrespective of the hour has woke me from my slumber.
Then I get mad when I am told, "The caller has withheld their number."

Wheelie-Bins

Now where do I put that old bucket? I don't know, though really I should.
It's clearly a plastic container, though the handle is metal and wood.
I think it should go in the blue bin,
But my neighbour does not think that's right.
He said it can't be re-cycled
And therefore should go in the white.

I'm told that 'green waste' from the garden should go in the yellow bin now,
Which places me in a dilemma, and brings a fresh crease to my brow.
When leaves from the trees in the garden in autumn come spiralling down,
They have mostly lost their green colour, and are generally yellow or brown.

Are slugs and snails deemed 'garden waste' or come under the term 'meat (uncooked)'.
I can't find them getting a mention in all of the lists I have looked.
The yellow bin is the most likely, though it possibly could be the blue.
I've received some conflicting advice and I really don't know what to do.

'Electrics' should go in the red bin. It was the last one to arrive.
But I'm not sure where I can put it. You see I now possess five.
My old radio's clearly electric but contained in a casing of wood.

I don't want to take them apart, though my neighbour insists that I should.

The green bin is solely for 'textiles'; that's where my old coat was to go.
"That's wrong," said my friend. "The collar's fur."
So what shall I do? I don't know.
Some tell me one bin is the right one while others insist that it's not.
So I'll take ev'rything to the garden, and bury the whole blooming lot!

Holidays

We're not off to Spain or Madeira again; air travel's become such a bore.
With all the delays, which might last for days we really can't stand any more.
We've nowhere to go, and we've let our friends know
We'll be spending our hols at Heathrow.

We know ev'ry shop and we'll spend till we drop, and enjoy all the goods there displayed.
We'll sleep on the floor as we've done before when our flight to New York was delayed.
The Mistral may blow, but we don't want to know for we're spending our hols a Heathrow.

We'll watch all the queues with their thoughts of cheap booze as they're off to some far-away places.
And we'll try to guess (though we couldn't care less) which travellers will lose their cases.
They'll find it a blow, but not us you must know for we're spending our hols at Heathrow.

We've no need to queue as the travellers do to check-in for days in the sun.
And when some kids riot and will not keep quiet we'll just sit and watch all the fun.
When skiers lack snow we don't want to know for we're spending our hols at Heathrow.

We've no need of sun-cream, as Spain's just a dream, and through Customs we've no need to go.
With no money to change we've no coins that are strange but just pounds, not a Franc or Euro.

We've no passports to show, for we've nowhere to go for we're spending our hols at Heathrow.

Baggage handlers may strike as long as they like, and we don't care a bit if they do.
And we won't give a hoot if flight crews follow suit and are joined by their cabin crews too.
And we'll just say *Heigh-Ho* if check-in staff go slow for we're spending our hols at Heathrow.

If there's a drawback, it's a serious lack of much nightlife in Terminal Three.
So it helps pass the night, when late-comers get tight and are banned from their flight to Capri.
We'll enjoy the aggro as we don't want to go, for we're spending our hols at Heathrow.

The Gardener

It's kind of you to say so, sir, I try to keep it neat
And colourful, because I think it brightens up the street.
I'm sure that it's important, sir, to keep front gardens bright,
With lots of different bedding plants and not a weed in sight.

But round the back it's different; the earth is mainly clay,
And it's hard to get a fork in if the weather's like today.
While it becomes a sea of mud if we get days of rain,
Then sticks like glue to spade and shoe and digging's quite a
strain.

We gard'ners often find it hard to keep a smiling face because
of countless pests that lurk in ev'ry hiding place.
We must prepare for set-backs too, for sometimes in the spring
An unexpected late frost comes and ruins ev'rything.

For it's hard work in a garden; I've had my share of shocks
Like when the slugs ate all the tops of my prize hollyhocks,
And caterpillars munched their way at an enormous pace,
Through leaves of cabbages and sprouts until they looked like
lace.

I've found wireworm in my turnips and maggots in the peas,
And brown rot's spreading rapidly through apples in the trees.
There are greenfly on my roses and blackfly on my beans;
I can't seem to get rid of them, though I've tried many means.

There's mildew on the marrows, and some pests I cannot name
Have ruined my begonias; it really is a shame.
I've mares' tails in the flower beds which spread at quite a rate,
And bindweed in the borders that I can't eradicate.

It's time I cut the grass again, though quite a lot of clover
As well as moss and dandelions seem to have taken over.
You must agree, a gard'ners life is hard and full of strife,
But I'm happy in the garden – out of earshot of my wife.

Church Service

Our Vicar is a trendy chap, to go-ahead some fear,
For if you phone the Vic'rage now this message you will hear.
"We welcome you to our fine Church built in fifteen forty-three.
For your convenience just note these options carefully.

To book a wedding in the Church you should press button ONE,
And say if you would like the choir or have the Church bells rung.
Though if it's rather urgent, then you should press button TWO;
Just leave your name and number and I'll soon get back to you.

You'll hear my latest sermon if you now press button THREE,
And learn how Moses came to serve his people faithfully,
We're short of helpers in the Church, and we could do with more.
If you can serve by cleaning brass or dusting pews, press FOUR.

The Organ Fund is falling short, however much we strive;
To learn a way that you can help please now press button FIVE.
We've wet rot in the rafters, and a leaking roof to fix.
We can take gifts by credit cards if you press button SIX.

If you feel you can organise our Church's fete press SEVEN.
A thankless task but you will get a just reward in Heaven.
Weddings and Christenings combined are charged a special rate;
If this is something you require, please now press button EIGHT.

Our Treasurer, it's sad to say, is shortly to resign.
To get a worthwhile (unpaid) job, and you can count, press NINE.
If further details of our Church activities are sought,
And times of our Church services, then please press button NOUGHT.

We've plenty more to offer you which will suit ev'ry age.
You'll find more information on our Parish web-page.
If you can spare a little time it would be nice to see
You at some of our services, even occasionally.

After The Flood

Noah to his wife one day confided,
"It seems the waters have subsided,
And as dry land I now can see,
The animals can be set free."
His wife replied, "That's just as well;
Their quarters have a dreadful smell.
I didn't think we'd be so long;
It really is an awful pong.
If you think I'll clear up their mess,
You'd better have another guess."
Noah said, "There is no need to shout.
Don't fret yourself. They'll soon be out."
Then to his charges then said Noah,
"I shortly will unlock the door,
And you'll be free. I'll say good-bye;
You must go forth and multiply;
But I implore you, curb your passion,
And leave us in an ordered fashion."
But through the door the creatures rushed,
And Noah was very nearly crushed,
As elephants and hippos tried
To exit quickly side by side.
But they were gone eventually,
Leaving Noah with his family.
Then to his wife and sons said Noah,
"The ark's not wanted anymore;
So let's away; the weather's grand,
And we must go and till the land."
Noah's youngest son was wont to shirk
The slightest form of manual work;
And said to Noah, "Why must we go?
I do not want to plough and sow.

I'm sure the ark still has its uses;
Let's advertise it for spring cruises."
Noah snorted. "That's absurd," said he.
"How would you get it to the sea?"
So out they went, but then Noah found
Two snakes nearby upon the ground.
And full of wrath, he gave a shout.
"I told you when I let you out
You must go out and multiply,
But you're still here; just tell me why."
The snakes replied, "Don't make a fuss;
It's very difficult for us.
To multiply is hard for we
Are simple adders, can't you see."

The Book Case

I needed a new bookcase and I saw one on display.
It was just what I wanted so I bought it straight away.
I knew just where to put it, so I cleared a corner space,
And duly made a note of when delivery would take place.

That day a cardboard box arrived. My goodness that was IT!
There was no doubt that I had bought a self-assembly kit!
I tipped the contents on the floor, then found a note which said
"Do not unpack the parts 'til the instructions you have read."

The instruction book I found at last beneath the turned-out pile.
It said 'First check the contents' and this took me quite a while,
For all the items on the list were spread around the floor.
I couldn't tell if all were there, or if there should be more.

So I decided it was best to start assembling it,
And find the items as required to get the parts to fit.
Page one of the instructions read: "Make sure before you start
That you have all the tools you need, and ev'ry bookcase part."

It listed tools which seemed to be essential for the job.
"A spirit level, setsquare and a decorator's bob;
Screwdrivers (Philips) large and small, a hammer, clamps and
drill."
And said assembly of the parts require but little skill.

Although I know I've little skill, the rest left me dismayed.
I do not own such tools as I'm no workman I'm afraid.
As I can't be the only one without those tools at hand
There must be ways of tackling it the makers hadn't planned.

Instructions told me that the parts should be joined up by screwing;
I wondered if, instead of screws, they could be held by gluing.
So I got out my strongest glue and stuck the parts by that.
But the finished bookcase makes an odd addition to my flat.

The sides are at an angle and the top is not quite true;
The shelves all slope towards the right despite excess of glue.
It really is unique although you'd hardly call it smart,
Though I tell my visitors that it's expensive modern art.

It is moreover fragile and will not support my books,
But as it makes a talking point I'll keep it for its looks.
So I still need a bookcase for my books strewed round the floor,
But not a self-assembly kit I'm absolutely sure!

The Wallyphant

A zoo-keeper, Jack Bolliphant,
Was first to breed a wallyphant,
But even he has to confess
It wasn't really a success.
Jack looked after the elephant house.
He liked the job but had one grouse.
His early morning task was then
To clean the creature's sleeping den.
But first had to get them outside
Ready for visitors to ride.
Due to their slow and lumbering gait
Invariably he finished late.
"It's clear," he thought, "There is a need
For some way to increase their speed."
He pondered long, then said, "I see,
I'll cross one with a wallaby.
Their offspring will then leap about
And lead the others quickly out."
(He would have said a kangaroo,
But there was not one at the zoo.)
But when Wal wallyphant was born
Ma elephant eyed it with scorn.
And Jack himself was rather wrought;
It didn't look as he had thought.
The creature hadn't got a trunk;
Its proboscis had clearly shrunk.
It wasn't like a trunk at all;
More like a well-used tennis ball.
It had a tiny tail, what's more;
Not like a wallaby's he saw.
Pa wallaby said, "It's plain to see
The lad does not take after me."

And Wal, with a bewildered air,
Wondered what he was doing there,
And trying to hop from place to place
Fell flat on his truncated face.
And as Wal couldn't leap or hop,
Jack knew his idea was a flop.
He's learnt his lesson now, I wager.
It's tricky to tamper with nature.
God gave to all his divers' creatures
Distinguished individual features
And though we're meant to use our skill
We tamper with nature at our peril.

The Malady

(This was written at a time when there seemed to be a very long run-up to the 2012 Olympics)

"I thought my husband was just lazy,
But now I'm sure that he's gone crazy.
Impervious to my derision
He sits before the television
And watches it for hours on end.
I'm sure that he is round the bend,
For all he does is sit and stare,
And rarely rises from his chair.
With barely time for lunch or tea
He hurries back to his TV.
And every day is just the same,
So Doctor that is why I came
To see you, hoping you could say
What makes him act in that strange way?
And tell me that you could restore
Him back to normal health once more."

"My dear, don't worry for you see,
It's not a serious malady
But just a trivial condition
Allied to modern television.
No need for treatment as I'm sure
Time will produce a total cure.
Your husband's case is not unique;
I saw another just last week.
In front of the TV he sticks
In training for the Olympics."

The Object

A caveman chipped at a stone he'd found
Until it was completely round.
Then chipped a hole in the stone's dead centre
Large enough for a stick to enter.
To his delight the caveman found
That on the stick the stone went round,
He said, "Look what I have done"
As on the stick the stone he spun.
His father said, "Don't waste your time |
On such a frivolous pastime.
That object that you showed me can
Have no good use for beast nor man.
Throw it away and be so good
As to help me shift this load of wood."
What happened next upon that day
So long ago it's hard to say,
As cavemen, though in some ways bright,
Had not acquired the skill to write.
And so we'll never know... I feel
If a caveman did invent the wheel.
As all we're left is an unsolved riddle
Of a circular stone with a hole in the middle.

The English

Two Englishmen abroad may sometimes bother
To remark on the weather
Or nod to each other.
But will never, ever, dine together unless they've been
introduced

Brief Encounter

I'm sure I'd eaten far too much upon last Christmastide,
With turkey, all the trimmings, and with nibbles on the side.
To lose the weight I must have gained I thought I'd take a run,
And didn't pass another soul enjoying the wintry sun.
But then I spied a stranger sat upon a wayside seat,
And thought that I would join him there to rest my weary feet.
He took no notice as I sat, and seemed in deepest thought.
I didn't like to disturb him if solitude he sought.
I watched the stranger as he sat in silent contemplation, and
wondered how he came to be in such a situation.
For he wore ancient trousers and an older coat on top,
As if picked up at random from a local charity shop.
Then suddenly the stranger spoke with accent rather queer.
I found it hard to place it, but he didn't come from here.
"Do you believe in ghosts?" he said, much to my consternation.
It was, I thought, the strangest way to start a conversation
"I don't," I said in my reply. "I think that you will find
They're visions conjured up within a weak disordered mind."
The stranger gave a sigh and said, "It is just as I feared.
A pity as I am one." as he slowly disappeared.

The Invention

Bill Henson in Victoria's reign
Designed a steam-powered aeroplane,
And went and asked the Government
To help in its development.
Though Bill had patented his scheme
They weren't enamoured by his dream,
And said, "What! Fly like a bird?
The whole idea is quite absurd.
You certainly have got a cheek
And must think we were born last week.
Your airy project, we are sure,
Can have no use in peace or war."
And though Bill did his very best
It was quite clear they weren't impressed.
"You'll get no cash from us," said they,
So Bill, much saddened, went away.
The flat rejection he took hard,
And went back to his home in Chard,
And never, ever, worked again
On his envisaged aeroplane.
Some sixty years or so went by,
And though some others tried to fly,
It wasn't 'til the brothers Wright
Made their recorded first powered flight.
But if some money had been found,
And got Bill's project off the ground,
It could in, 1843,
Have changed the course of history.

Surprisingly, the events depicted in the above rhyme are basically true. William Samuel Henson, to give him his full name, was born in May 1812 and trained as an engineer. He worked initially in the lace-making industry, which was rapidly becoming mechanised at the time, and made a number of improvements in lace- making machines. However, he had wide and varied interests, and besides his involvement in flying machines, he designed some light-weight steam engines, and patented the first T-shaped razor, later taken up by Gillette and others.

The Aerial Steam Carriage, as he called it, as the word Aeroplane had not, at the time come into existence, was developed in conjunction with a colleague by the name of John Stringfellow. The machine, as proposed, was a monoplane having a cambered wing with a wing-span of 150 feet (roughly half as long again as that of a Lancaster) and was to have been driven by two contra-rotating propellers powered by a specially designed light-weight 50 horse-power liquid-fuelled steam engine.

On failing to get Government funding, Henson, with Stringfellow and others, formed a company which they called The Aerial Transit Company in an endeavour to get sufficient funds to develop the Steam Carriage. The elaborate and fanciful prospectus showed passengers being transported as far afield as Egypt, India and China and this was before a full scale flying machine had been built and tested. However they failed to get the necessary money, as the proposal seemed to be too far-fetched, the press at the time being particularly sceptical.

On failure of the company, the dejected Henson with his family emigrated to The United States where he continued to make inventions, one of which being an ice-making machine, but as far as is known, he never worked on a flying machine again. He died in1888 and was buried in New Jersey.

In this country John Stringfellow continued to design various forms of aircraft,

Including bi-planes and tri-planes but these were also unsuccessful. He died in 1883.

However the Aerial Steam Carriage was not just a pie-in-the-sky idea as Henson was clearly aware of the principles of flight. His proposed machine had a rudder and elevator in the tail to control the aircraft's movement in the air just like later flying machines and the patented design had a number of constructional features which were incorporated in some early flying aircraft up to and including the First World War. It is interesting to note that the method of imparting the drive from the engine to the propellers as proposed by Henson was, in fact, basically the same as that later used by the Wright brothers in their first aircraft. Clearly the failure of Henson's design was due to the fact that steam engines, even the proposed light-weight ones, did not have a sufficiently high power-to-weight ratio, and it wasn't until the invention of petrol engines that powered flight became a practicable proposition.

So despite failing to produce the first actual powered flying machine, William Samuel Henson should be more widely remembered for his pioneering contributions to aircraft design.

The Anniversary

Next week is our Church Anniversary
And a Church full of flowers I'd like to see,
So bring them along next Saturday
To make a really eye-dazzling display.
This caught the attention of youngster Jack
Who sat with his parents at the back,
Now awake (though he'd slept the sermon through),
And he thought he would see what he could do.
So on Saturday morning Jack spent hours
Collecting the best of some mixed wild flowers,
Then went to the Church just after his lunch
And offered a flower arranger his bunch
"I cannot use those," young Jack heard her say.
"They're no good to me. Please take them away."
The Vicar, just afterwards passing by
Caught sight of a tear in the youngster's eye.
And so he said, "What's the matter my lad?
Why is it that you are looking so sad?"
Jack answered, "I brought flowers for the display,
But they said they're no good so take them away."
"I'm sure" said the Vicar "there's some mistake,
So come with your flowers and I will take
You to our store and we shall borrow
A vase to show off your flowers tomorrow,
And I'll put them upon our Altar rail
So everyone can see them without fail."
He did just that, and Jack went away
Happier then than earlier that day.
Considering next day's sermon that night,
The Vicar's first thought was the widow's mite,
But wondered instead if the theme should be
Suffer little children to come to me.

But then a solution came to mind.
"I'm sure," he thought, "these could be combined."
So this he did, and on Sunday he
Delivered his sermon eloquently.
But Jack slept through the Vicar's oration
Not knowing he was its inspiration.
Though that day he slept with a smiling face
For the flowers he'd brought had pride of place.

The Party

The Christmas party was well under way;
The guests all determined to enjoy their day;
They'd eaten well, and were now waiting for
What evening activities there were in store.
The hosts had been fortunate to obtain
A well-known magician to entertain,
So the guests settled down to watch the show,
With a young boy in the very front row.
A puff of smoke; the guests all cheered
As from the smoke the magician appeared.
"I'm known as Howdini," he said, "and I
Aim to intrigue you and mystify."
But the magician's first trick had hardly begun
When the boy in the front said, "I know how it's done."
And after each trick, again and again
'I know how it's done' came the same refrain.
The magician seemed to be getting mad,
But to the boy he said mildly, "My lad,
I see you're bright and very quick,
Could you help me with my very next trick?"
The boy, it was clear was very impressed,
For he, very speedily, acquiesced.
The magician found a kitchen chair,
And said to the boy, "Will you please sit there.
Just keep very still, and don't make a sound."
And quickly pulled a curtain around.
Then drew it away at the count of three,
And the chair was empty as all could see.
The boy had obviously disappeared,
And the gathered guests all clapped and cheered.
The magician bowed to the loud applause.
The guests clearly thought he had good cause.

He continued the show quite unperturbed,
As if by the boy he'd not been disturbed.
And then he finally finished the show,
Though the guests did not want to let him go.
For they all agreed with tumultuous cheers,
It was the best party they'd been to for years.
What became of the boy no-one can say,
For he hasn't been seen since that party day,
Though some of the guests claim they heard him say
"I know how it's d…" as he vanished away.

The Rug

"I think the new rug's extra long." my true love said to me,
And seeing it upon the floor I had but to agree.
I couldn't understand it, as I'm usually precise,
And to be absolutely sure I'd measured the old one twice.
I still recall the paper that I took to the shop with me,
And on that paper written down was clearly six and three.
Then suddenly, out of the blue, the answer came to me.
It wasn't six foot three at all,
But inches sixty-three.
You do not have to tell me that I wouldn't have been confused
If, in place of feet and inches, metric units I had used.
After events have taken place
It's easy to be wise;
But where millimetres are used for dimensions I find
It's hard to envisage the size.

King Wenceslas Revisited

We're told King Wenceslas looked out one freezing winter's night,

And saw a poor man gath'ring fuel under the moon's bright light.

The King took pity on the man, and to his Page, he said

"We'll take him a huge food parcel, so he'll be fully fed."

So they took stacks of food and wine to that poor man's rough shack,

And to his Page King Wenc'las said, "Now nothing he need lack."

Next day the King again looked out as he had done before.

Surprised, he saw the same poor man was trespassing once more.

"Call out the guard," King Wenc'las cried, "and bring that man to me,

And I will tell him that henceforth the firewood isn't free."

"Good sir," the poor man said to him, "my family's still in need.

In my poor hovel o'er the hill I've fourteen mouths to feed.

As you may guess I find that life

Is very hard today,

With wife and thirteen children, and another on the way.

So we would like more flesh and wine, if your good Kingship pleases;

A few plum puddings would be fine, as well as some choice cheeses."

"You must," the King said, "understand. If I gave more to you,

Then all my subjects in the land would want to have some too.

So you must find another one who those provisions gives.

But I'll give what you clearly need; a box of contraceptives.

Progress? Or Journey's End

Late afternoon one bright October day,
A band of walkers trudged their weary way.
To cheer the walkers on, their Leader said,
"The goal we seek is not that far ahead.
Just o'er the hill and by a wood you'll see
'The Golden Lion' an ancient hostelry."
And as a spur, as he'd been there before,
He regaled them of many treats in store.
"Once we're inside and shed our haversacks,
Around a roaring fire we can relax,
And rest our feet while sampling local ales
Or if you wish their legend'ry cocktails.
And then to us they'll bring a menu vast
For each to choose their favourite repast,
With choicest wines brought from their cellar's store.
I don't think you could ever wish for more.
From walking you'll enjoy that brief respite,
And I am sure they'll bed us for the night.
So every one of us will surely say,
'A perfect ending to an autumn day'."
But as they reached the top of the last hill,
The walker's leader suddenly stood still.
And looked before him in complete surprise.
Just wondering if he could believe his eyes.
For where the inn had nestled by the wood,
A new-built block of flats now clearly stood.

The Proposal

In silence the young couple sat together hand in hand,
Oblivious of the crowded room, the singer and the band.
Although the young man would have liked to stay like that all day,
He had some words upon his mind that he'd proposed to say.
"Shall we – that is to say – will you?" the young man shyly said,
And as he spoke he felt his face was slowly turning red.
"Of course! I thought you'd never ask." quickly the girl replied.
"I'll have fillet steak, mushrooms and chips with salad on the side."

The First Visit to the Dentist

"This won't hurt, sonny," the dentist said
As he helped me into his chair,
"So don't be afraid," he then went on, but I wished myself
elsewhere.

"Just open your mouth," he said to me. I reluctantly complied.
"You'll not feel a thing," he then remarked,
But I felt the dentist lied.

"It won't hurt a bit," he said again, but I felt no urge to linger.
'I'm sure this will' was my reply, as I bit his probing finger.

Odds and Ends

Harold's hearing's rather bad,
Which often made his loved one mad.
When he was asked to buy some carrots,
He came home with a pair of parrots;
Which on his wife was rather rough
As both the birds proved old and tough.

A female 'Student of the Year'
Was not so bright as might appear.
She, thinking it was quite a feat,
Designed a new ejector seat.
But someone really should have stopped her
Trying it out on a helicopter.

A land developer in town
Tripped on a kerb and tumbled down.
A passer-by who saw him fall
Said, "There's another urban sprawl."

As I was going to St Ives
I met a man with seven wives.
He said to me, "It should be well,
But I've seven mothers-in-law as well."

As I was staying in St Ives
I saw that man with seven wives.
"With paternity leave for each," said he,
"I'm now on holiday permanently."

Animal Crackers

If you should meet some crocodiles
Be wary of their cordial smiles.
They may appear a friendly bunch
But only look on you as lunch.

Porcupines have prickly spines and tempers too to match 'em.
So do take care thick gloves to wear: if you set out to catch 'em.

Chimpanzees climb trees with ease, and cats will sometimes
dare to.
But voles and moles prefer their holes, and rabbits seldom care
to.

When swimming should you meet a shark, no need to be polite.
Ignore an invitation to join it in a bite.
Don't stop to say 'How do you do?', 'Good Morning' or 'Good
Day'.
Pretend you have another date, and quickly swim away.

The wise old owl sat in an oak.
The more he heard, the less he spoke.
The less he spoke, the more he heard.
But wasn't he a boring bird?

Tortoises are quite sedate
And walk at a slow and steady rate.
Unlike the restless hares in spring
That dash around like anything.

The platypus is quite absurd,
Being partly a mammal and partly a bird

Rabbits cannot add,
But multiply like mad.

When he's commuting Sir Jeremy Monk
Always takes with him Jemima his skunk.
His pet ensures that they have, he explains,
Plenty of space for themselves on the trains.

Why is it that nobody loves the slug.
It doesn't rob banks and it's not known to mug.
It won't spray graffiti on somebody's wall,
Smash windows of shops or take part in a brawl.
It never joy rides in a car that's not taxed,
And won't pick a quarrel – it's far too relaxed.
It won't stone the police or incite a riot,
And on the whole it's remarkably quiet.
I'm sure you'll agree that the slug is not bad,
So I can't understand why it's unloved and sad.
You have no idea how sad I would be
If I were a mollusc and no-one loved me.
As nobody loves them I don't find it queer
That slugs drown their sorrows in saucers of beer.

When baby turtles first emerge they hurry to the sea,
And travel many thousand miles until maturity.
And after many years at sea with inborn skill unmatched,
They travel back unerringly to the beach where they were
hatched.
Just how they find their way is nature's unsolved mystery,
For clearly they do not have maps or signposts in the sea.
I wonder how they manage it for often when I roam,
I can get lost completely even when not far from home.

Section III

The Moral Muse

Nelly

This is the tale of little Nelly
Who ate a quite enormous jelly
And though it wasn't really wise
She followed it with ten mince pies.
Then just in case she'd lost some weight
She piled some trifle on her plate.
And after that she thought she'd try
A largish slice of apple pie,
With cream, of course, two inches thick;
It made her neighbours feel quite sick.
And that was only just the start;
She had to try some treacle tart,
And sausage rolls – just three or four –
To leave some room for something more
Exciting, like the strawberry flan,
Or crepes Suzettes straight from the pan.
The gateau, too, was rather nice
So Nelly took another slice.
And steadily with moving jaws
She munched away with scarce a pause.
Her mother, who was standing near,
Said, "Easy on the mince pies, dear."
But Nelly, not to be deterred,

Started upon her twenty-third.
Then tried to rise, but was not able,
And slowly slid beneath the table.
Then plaintively from on the floor
A voice said, "Can I have some more
Of the delightful c…" then BOOM;
A loud explosion shook the room;
Just like a sudden clap of thunder
Nell's party dress had burst asunder.
Like stranded whale upon the shore
She lay recumbent on the floor,
Regretting she'd not time to take
A second slice of cherry cake.
You do not need me to explain;
The moral of this tale is plain.
Unless you want to be like Nelly
You should not start a meal with jelly.

Emily

This is the tale of Emily
Who climbed into an apple tree,
And though her mother said, "Come down."
She merely answered with a frown.
Ignoring consequences dire
She clambered upwards even higher.
Her father said, "It's plain to see
She thinks she is a chimpanzee.
We obviously need some aid.
I'll go and call the Fire Brigade."
The firemen rushed there from the station
And quickly grasped the situation.
As Emmy swung from bough to bough
The Fire Chief mopped his wrinkled brow.
Shielding his eyes from sunlight's glare
He said, "She shouldn't be up there.
But though we'd like to help restore
Your daughter to the ground once more,
Our longest ladders are at a fire
And all the rest are out on hire.
To get her down, it's plain to see
We'll have to fell your apple tree."
"You can't do that," said Emmy's poppa
"That Cox's is a heavy cropper."
"Then we'll be off," the Fire Chief said,
Putting his helmet on his head.
"I'm sorry that we cannot stay;
We've six more calls to make today.
Here is my card; just give a ring;
We'll turn our hand to anything.
Hours nine to twelve and two 'til four."
Then in their engine off they tore.

As Emmy waved the men good-bye,
Her mother gave a little sigh,
And making a despairing plea
Said, "Emmy, don't you want your tea?"
But Emmy, though she clearly heard,
Pretended that she was a bird.
Up there she stayed for days on end,
Despite entreaties to descend.
She missed her breakfasts, teas and dinner,
And slowly she became much thinner,
Until a blackbird overhead
Saw Emily below, and said,
"A caterpillar I declare."
And swooped upon her from the air.

Ignoring Emmy's loud protest
He carried her off to his nest.

The moral of this little rhyme
Is – if a tree you want to climb –
Think of the fate of Emily
Getting as thin as thin can be
And ending up a blackbird's snack,
So don't forget some food to pack!

William

Young William gave his parents fits
As he liked to take things to bits,
And though he tried with might and main
He couldn't put them back again
Precisely as they were before,
Which really made his parents sore.
One day the bathroom scales he spied
And thought that he would look inside.
He worked as fast as he was able
And soon had parts spread on the table.
But when young William put them back
He clearly didn't have the knack,
For though he tried the best he could
They didn't function as they should.
The scales, no longer accurate,
Showed William ten pounds overweight;
His mother said "You're much too stout,
So chips and chocolate are out.
Until I see you getting thinner
It's lettuce only for your dinner."

The cuckoo clock within the kitchen
Once set young William's fingers itching,
And when his mother was in town
He soon had fetched the timepiece down.
Enthusiastic'lly he started,
And case and works were quickly parted.
With screws removed out came the springs,
And wheels and countless other things
Whose function William couldn't guess.
It was a most untidy mess.
So, interest upon the wane,

He thought he'd put them back again,
But some he clearly overlooked,
As cuckoo "oo'd" before it "cuck'd"
And hands went round at quite a rate,
Soon indicating half past eight,
Though really it was just past four.
Then William's father came and saw
The clock, and to his son he said,
"Upstairs at once; it's time for bed."

Once William's Grandpa came to stay,
And thought he'd take a nap one day.
He put his watch down by his side
Which William very quickly spied;
And when his grandpa was asleep
He thought that he would take a peep.
"It cannot do much harm," said he
As he took off the back to see
What made the hands go round and round,
And then he very quickly found
A knob that he could turn, also
A lever that moved to and fro.
He would have liked to see much more,
But as his grandpa ceased to snore
And seemed that he must soon awaken,
Will put the watch from where 'twas taken.
Later that day Will's grandpa said,
"I'll take you to the Circus lad.
Just get your coat and come with me;
The circus starts at half past three."
They reached the ticket office, but
They found that it was firmly shut.
A man said, "You're late for the show.
It's nearly six o'clock you know."
Said grandpa, "Are you really sure?
My watch was never wrong before.
The man said "I'm afraid it's so.

You two have really missed the show.
This evening we shall pack the tent;
Tomorrow we'll be down in Kent."
The moral is, no doubt you'll see,
Without requiring help from me,
With grandpa's watch don't interfere
When there's a circus showing near.

Carrie

Young Carrie, on the plumpish side,
Was carried by the ebbing tide
Away from land, and out to sea,
Far from her loving family.
Now Captain John and brother Jack
Were sailing in their fishing smack,
When suddenly to John, Jack said,
"I think there is a whale ahead."

So to his Captain Jack said, "Let
Us catch the creature in our net."
They acted then with one accord
To bring their quarry soon aboard.
Then John and Jack said, "Glory be
That's not a whale, but a girl we see."
And they could only stand and stare
As she, recumbent, gasped for air.

Then John said to his brother Jack,
"I think we'll have to put her back;
We've now more than our quota caught;
And cannot take her into port.
They're bound to fine us if they see
How much we've netted, and maybe
They'll confiscate our vessel too,
And then I don't know what we'd do."

Jack said, "Let's sail 'til nearer land
And put her in the water, and
Let her swim a little more
Until she's safely on the shore."
To her the brothers then expressed

Their plan, at which she acquiesced.
All that she wanted was to be
United with her family.

She swam as the two brothers planned
And very soon was on the land.
She met a stranger on the shore
Who said to her, "Cherie, bonjour."
She realised, by choice or chance,
She'd been put down in northern France.
So she returned the salutation,
And explained to him the situation.
She told the man she met that she
Had started swimming in the sea,
And started from a place called Dover.
"I'm glad," she said, "the ordeal's over."
But didn't mention that (you'll note)
She'd travelled some way in a boat.

"So back to Dover I must go."
He said, "C'est difficile, you know."
We're now near Calais, so you've swum
La Manche cherie, so with me come
To see the Mayor who'd like to meet
A young girl who'd done such a feat."
The Mayor kissed Carrie on the cheek,
And said to her, "C'est magnifique."

And Carrie, aware of the confusion,
Did not the Frenchmen disillusion.
The Mayor kissed Carrie once again
And said, "Come with me to my plane,
And I will fly you back to see
You home with all your family."
And so he did and told them he
Admired Carrie enormously
For what she'd done, and to this day

What really happened she'll not say,

But very soon her fam'ly made
The most of Carrie's escapade.
A story in the local press
Called her a heroine, no less.
A national paper heard it too,
And asked her for an interview,
They paid her well, and she
Gained further notoriety.

So Carrie, with no sense of shame
Revelled in undeserved fame,
And on the television she
Was hailed as a celebrity.
This story has a moral too.
I'm sure that it's not lost on you.
If fate gives you a helping hand
Do not let on it wasn't planned.

Section IV

Love sonnets

My Very First Love

You held me safe in your enfolding arm.
I was content to know that you were near;
Your presence was a shield against all harm,
And helped to stifle ev'ry foolish fear.
You gave me hope when my own faith was low,
And strength when signs of weakness you could see;
Encouragement when doubts began to show,
And will to overcome adversity.
You praised my efforts even when I'd failed,
And comforted me in times of pain and grief.
You gave me courage when I might have quailed,
And taught me discipline and self-belief.
Since you departed I have found no other
To equal you, my first love; yes, my mother.

First Love

Her golden hair haloed a smiling face,
I'd never seen, I thought, a lovelier sight,
And by my side she spied an empty place
At which she sat, and set my heart alight.
Our days together passed as if on wings;
We shared our hopes, and secret fears confessed;
We laughed as one at countless silly things,
And comforted each other when distressed.
And when she spoke I hung on ev'ry word;
I was content, but life can be unfair;
For as we ended our first year I heard
We were to go to sep'rate schools elsewhere.
To say, "Let's still be friends." I had no chance;
She left without a wave or backward glance.

Lost Love

I treasure, still, the mem'ries of those days,
Now long since passed, when blissful times we shared.
The fleeting years cannot, for me, erase
The thoughts of everlasting love declared.
I can't forget, despite the mounting years,
Since those far days when youthful ardour burned,
Of times we whispered secrets in each other's ears,
And mutual fears and aspirations learned.
Some sleepless nights I conjure up your face,
And wonder if you've memories as well
Of times we walked through woods in close embrace,
And laughed together under Cupid's spell.
And then my love for you I had to smother,
When you, perversely, went and chose another.

Section V

The New Canterbury Tales

The Tabard Inn in Southwark is renowned
As resting place for many pilgrims bound
For Canterbury some way to the East
To see the place where Thomas the Archpriest
Was murdered as he at the altar bowed;
Though others merely came to join the crowd
For company along The Old Kent Road,
And points beyond like Rochester and Strood.
For many reasons to the inn they went
To join the pilgrims on their way to Kent.

So as the pilgrims started on their way
They weren't the only travellers that day.
A group (all parties) of MPs was there;
Their self-important braying filled the air.
Each spoke in banal clichés all the day,
Not list'ning to what others had to say.
Each Member only by himself impressed,
Appointed to his first fact-finding quest
(With all expenses paid) his time to spend
Looking for ways that he could recommend
For regulating pilgrims as they went
Towards their goal in Canterbury, Kent.

And News Reporters gathered by the score;
There really wasn't room for any more.
All eager to be off but even keener
To be the first to find some misdemeanour
Committed by a person of high station,
And with some fanciful elaboration
Get it reported in the Sunday Press,
All in, they'll claim, the public interest.
And some, to boost their paper's circulation,
Were quite prepared to use imagination
To write, as far as libel laws allowed,
Of some (un-named) figure in the crowd,
Implying some dark secret in past life
Connected with another trav'llers wife.

Accountants joined the jolly crowd as well;
But just how many none of them could tell.
Each made a count but they could not agree;
Some made it thirty, others thirty-three;
But as some tax-inspectors might arrive
They quickly compromised on twenty-five.

It soon appeared they had not come for fun
So as in a crowd there's bus'ness to be done,
And pilgrims in the main are far too lax
To claim allowances against their tax.

And each accountant (for an ample fee)
Was eager to explain quite lengthily
How pilgrims who had bus' ness on the way
Could claim for miles they travelled ev'ry day,
With costs of their essential transportation,
Together with each year's depreciation.
And board and lodging they could claim as well
As shown on the receipts from each hotel.

Some Lawyers, too, were not to be outdone
And thought they'd also like to join the fun.
And all of them were swift to realise
That in a crowd disputes could oft arise.
So they were keen to tell each one they saw
Disputes could best be solved by Courts of Law.
And accidents in crowds could happen too,
And lawyers can advise on what to do,
For there must always be someone to blame,
And they know just how much victims can claim
If they can only persuade them to sue
(With eyes upon the fees they'll charge it's true).
Those taking action might be out of pocket,
The lawyers, then, the only ones to profit.

Insurance Agents, too, were there in force
With many application forms of course,
To cover each eventuality,
From earthquakes and the loss of life at sea,
And ev'ry like calamitous event
Which might befall a traveller in Kent.
Each Agent urging pilgrims to make sure
They're covered against ailments quite obscure
That they might be infected with enroute;
All vying with each other to recruit
New clients, off'ring gifts if they would sign
At once their names upon the dotted line.
The policies on paper very grand
Were very difficult to understand,
With all exclusion clauses writ so small
As to escape the sharpest eyes of all.
The Agents there appeared to have one mission,
Which was, it seems, to earn the most commission.

A clutch of taxi-drivers, too, was there;
Each hoping to pick up a wealthy fare
Who would accept without a single question

The statement that there was severe congestion
On the A2 at Rochester, which meant
A detour round another part of Kent,
Through Winchelsea and Rye and Deal and Sturry
To reach their final goal in Canterbury.
So many ventured to the inn that day,
To join the pilgrims as they went their way.
The Tabard's host, a very striking figure,
(Though small his manner made him seem much bigger)
Greeted ev'ry trav'ller to his inn
As long-lost friends or homeward-coming kin.
"Come in," he'd say. "You're more than welcome here.
My inn is stocked with finest wines and beer;
The best in town. You're new this way, I see;
I trust you're well and all your family."
He welcomed ev'ry pilgrim in that way,
And said that he would join them if he may,
And had a plan, he hoped they would agree,
To pass time and relieve monotony.
Said he, "There must be many who are able
To tell some story, parable or fable,
And to the one who tells the finest tale
I'll give a keg of Tabard's choicest ale.
I'll be the judge, so who will be the first
To try to win the means to quench their thirst?"
A young accountant, coveting the ale,
Was first to volunteer to tell a tale.
"Good lad," the host cried, "let us on our way.
We'll listen carefully to what you say."

The Accountant's Tale

A bus'ness man played golf with friends each week
And said one day "Please don't think it's a cheek.
I'll lend to each five thousand pounds," he said,
"to drop within my grave when I am dead.
For where I'm going nobody can say,
But I must be prepared as best I may,
And do not wish to travel on that day
Without some cash to help me on my way."
His friends, a doctor, banker and a priest
Said, "Do not worry. When your life has ceased, we are most
willing to perform that task;
It is a very simple thing you ask."
Eventually he died, and at his end,
The other three his fun'ral did attend,

And afterwards, with all the rites complete,
They to the nearest tavern did retreat.
Then to the others each of them expressed
What they had done about their friend's request.
The priest said he'd committed a grave sin,
As he had only put three thousand in,
And kept two thousand of the money lent.
"Not for myself," he said, "but to augment
The Church's building fund, because," he said,
"We must quite soon replace the roofing lead,
Or else the congregation will complain
Each time they are baptised with leaking rain.
Our friend would have agreed, I'm sure
For if he'd lived he would have given more."
The doctor then spoke up and did confess
That he, as well, had put in somewhat less.
A mere two thousand pounds. "The rest," he said,

"I'll give to the hospital instead.
Of medical equipment they are short,
And new expensive drugs need to be bought.
I'm certain that he would have acquiesced.
Of hospitals he had an interest."
Then spoke the banker to the other two,
"I'm disappointed gentlemen in you.
Examples to your fellows should be set,
And promised obligations should be met,
Despite the fact that dead men cannot count,
I've put a cheque in for the whole amount."

At this the Tabard's host laughed loud and said,
"It's hard to cash a cheque when you are dead.
That is a most amusing tale you've told.
Who's next among you who would be so bold
As to come forward and a story tell
To entertain us, hopefully as well
As did the brave accountant's merry tale,
And possibly secure my keg of ale."
At this an MP, not to be outdone,
Said, "I can tell a story of someone
Who had a strange experience one day.
I'll now recount what happened if I may."

The MP's Tale

He was a young election candidate
(Which party he belonged to I'll not state)
And visiting elector's votes to win,
One day to a hospital he went in
To show he cared for voters in distress.
(His visit carefully leaked to the press).
One man he saw was in a dreadful state.
He nearly was too bad to contemplate.
His head, except his eyes, completely bound
With bandages wound several times around.
Festooned with wires and tubes of ev'ry sort,
'Twas clear he could not eat the grapes he'd brought,
Or even talk, so it was hard to say
Who he'd be voting for on polling day.
But as his visitor was standing there
The patient tried to speak, but gasped for air.
He grabbed a writing pad and swiftly wrote,
And to his visitor he passed a note.
Then with the would-be MP by his side
The patient gave a final gasp and died.

The visitor stood for a while, perplexed,
And wondered what he should do next.
He clearly had the patient's last request,
But how important he could not have guessed,
For it was in a language quite unknown.
'Twas clear he could not read it on his own.
It certainly was neither French nor Greek.
A quick solution he would have to seek,
Because he knew that he would have no rest
Until he learned the patient's last request.
So to a knowledgeable friend he went

And told him of his strange predicament.
His friend said, "You were right to come to me;
This note is written in Chinese, I see;
A language that I know quite well.
Your patient's last request I soon will tell.
Although the writing's an awful mess,
And hard to read the patient's message says,
"Go back you stupidest of men.
You're standing on my pipe of oxygen."
Thus ends my tale, which tells you'll surely note
How a prospective MP lost a vote.

"Well done," the host said. "That was quite a tale:
It shows how well-intended plans can fail
With dire results. The man will not, it's plain,
Be canvassing in hospital again.
Now who'll be next with an experience
That they can share with our rapt audience."
A taxi-driver then spoke up. Said he,
"I have a tale; a strange one you'll agree.
It happened to me late one Christmas Eve;
It's one you'll not find easy to believe."
"I'm sure," the host said, "your lucidity
Will overcome our incredulity."

The Taxi Driver's Tale

That Christmas Eve I'd had a busy day,
And late that night was on my homeward way.
As I drove past a house in Welbeck Square
I saw a lonely figure standing there,
He beckoned me to stop, and when I did
He quickly clambered in, and then he bid
Me drive to Waterloo without delay.
He shut the door and we were on our way.
As I assumed that he had meant the station
I quickly set off for that destination,
But as we reached the bridge at Waterloo
The man said quietly to me "This will do."
I braked, but when I looked round for my fare,
I found that he had vanished in thin air.

I told another cabby who I knew
The tale I have imparted now to you.
He listened; then he said "Strange to relate,
I had the same experience quite late
One Christmas Eve some time ago. I went
Through Welbeck Square, and there I saw a gent waiting
outside a house beneath a lamp,
Quite oddly dressed. I thought he was a tramp.
He signalled me to stop. I did like you.
He also asked to go to Waterloo,
But when we got there and I looked around
My passenger was nowhere to be found.
Now some days later when I drove by chance
Through the same square I took a passing glance
At where the man had stood on that strange night.
I knew the spot because the lamp post's light
Had shone upon his cloak. I also saw

That night the house behind, and on the door
The number, plain as plain was twenty-six.
My eyes, I thought, must be playing tricks,
For of the house, by day, there was no trace;
An office block, I saw, was in its place.
I made enquiries and then I was told
The house became a ruin, and was sold
Some time ago, because the owner died;
It's said that he'd committed suicide
One Christmas Eve. Some neighbours saw him stand
Beneath the lamp, his action clearly planned.
Into a cab he climbed and was away,
And was not seen alive after that day.
His body by the River Police was found
At Lime house Reach, and he had clearly drowned.
That ends my story, and it will explain
Why I'll not go through Welbeck Square again.

The host said, "A strange tale, I'm sure,
For I've not heard of a ghost house before.
It is a most unusual apparition.
Now who'll be next to join my competition
And tell a tale of the mysterious
Or one that will amuse and cheer us.
Because, my friends, I really have to say
We've had enough of dying for today.
Surely there's someone in our grand parade
Who can tell a more lively escapade."
Then an insurance agent ventured, "Well,
A merrier tale than those I'll try to tell."

The Insurance Agent's Tale

The story's not my own I'll have you know.
It happened to a colleague long ago,
When he had started working as a youth.
He claimed the story was the gospel truth.
One day he was despatched to country farms
And told that he should use his youthful charms
To get reluctant farmers to take out
Insurances against heat stroke and drought.
But as he made his way to each farmyard
He found the task to be extremely hard.
The reason for it was not hard to seek
For it had poured with rain for all the week.
So finally the lad called it a day
Only to find that he had lost his way.
By chance he came across a cottage small
And thought that he would have to make a call
To ask directions, so he went and knocked.
A woman answered and she seemed most shocked
At what she saw, "You're soaking wet," she cried.
"You must dry off. So quickly come inside.
Sit by the fire. You're hungry too, I feel,
So when you've rested, join us in a meal."

After the lad was rested, dry and fed
They sat and chatted 'til the husband said,
"Young lad, I think you should be on your way.
We are afraid we can't ask you to stay;
You see we haven't any room for you.
Of bedrooms we have only two;
We sleep in one. Our daughter's in the other.
That's her, in yonder picture, with her mother."
He saw a pretty lass, some might say buxom,

With arms outstretched as if in welcome.
He longed to see and hold that daughter fair,
But, sad to say, the maiden was not there.
"She's gone to town tonight," the husband said,
"And won't be back until we are in bed."
His wife then said, "It really isn't kind
To turn the lad out. Do you think he'd mind
Sharing a bed with Blossom for tonight?"
"Young lad," said she, "there won't be any danger,
Though she can get quite friendly with a stranger.
If she gets very close, give her a clout,
Or she'll be on top of you ere night's out."
The lad could barely then avoid a grin.
"I'm happy and quite willing to fit in
With what you are proposing, ma'am," he said,
Imagining a lively night ahead,
And thought, "A perfect ending to the day."
"Come on," the man said. "I will lead the way."
He took him to an outhouse where he saw
What seemed to be a heaving mound of straw.
"What's that?" he thought, then heard the husband say,
"Come, Blossom lass, you've company today."
A head appeared with horns and yellow eyes,
As if it were the Devil in disguise.
And then the dreadful truth upon him smote.
He was to share his bedding with a goat!

"That's life," the host said, "always, there's a catch;
So never count your chickens 'til they hatch.
Can someone else come forward and regale
Us with another cautionary tale,
Or one to educate us or amuse?"
At this an ancient gatherer of news
Said, "I've a story that you might enjoy;
I heard it told when I was still a boy."

The Reporter's Tale

When the theatre critic was away
A cub reporter was sent to a play.
His editor gave him a clear instruction
To write a piece about a new production
Of 'Hamlet' played in modem dress, and so
That night to the theatre he did go.
He settled in the stalls and quickly saw
The play's no longer set in Elsinore,
But in a Middle Eastern town instead
Within a country still with King as head.
The words were still as Shakespeare wrote the play
So the reporter felt no need to stay.
He knew the play; he'd read it when at school,
And said, "To see the rest, I'd be a fool."
So after Hamlet's line, "ay, there's the rub."
He went to write his piece up in a pub.
His finished piece he thought a work of art
(Although imagination played a part)
And took it to his office at a sprint,
Eager to see his finished work in print.
So when his editor called him next day
The boy was quite expecting him to say
'Well done, my lad' or some such words of praise,
And possibly expecting him to raise
His salary, but found him full of ire.
"Why did you not report the dreadful fire
Which broke out in the last scene of Act III,
And caused the audience and cast to flee
From the theatre in a frenzied rush,
With many injuries caused by the crush
Of bodies reaching exits at a run.
Every other paper but this one

Prints the calamity on its front page;
Can you not wonder why I'm in a rage?
It is a case of blatant dereliction!
You're fired because it's facts I want, not fiction!"
So the reporter sadly went away;
His life, he thought, in ruins on that day.
And for a while he wished that he were dead,
But he had second thoughts that night in bed,
And, pondering what the editor had said,
He must, he felt, try something else instead.
So he decided to write fiction, and became
A leading nov'list in the land!

"That tale, too, has a moral," the host said.
"It shows, when life is dark, there's light ahead.
Life often takes a turn quite unexpected,
And not as one would like to have directed.
So who will be the next to entertain us
With tales of romance or of crimes most heinous?"
An aged lawyer then spoke up. Said he,
"You mentioned crime, and this reminded me
Of something which, when I was young, occurred.
The story's true. On this I give my word."

The Lawyer's Tale

Into a jeweller's shop a couple went,
To mark which was, to them, a great event.
They'd just become engaged and thought that they
Would buy a diamond ring that very day.
And as a serious choice had to be made,
Some rings upon the counter were displayed.
A petty criminal was just outside
And through the door the diamond rings he spied.
Not one to miss an opportunity,
And heeding not the likely penalty,
He sauntered in, got close to the display,
And swiftly grabbed a ring and was away.
Before the startled jeweller could shout, "Stop!"
The criminal had darted from the shop.
And though to stop him some brave person tried
He disappeared amongst the crowd outside.
The police soon came and many statements took.
A young PC said, "I know where to look.
The statements make it plain, and what is more
The thief left fingerprints upon the door.
The one who did this deed I know quite well.
His name is Joe and he lives in Camberwell.
I'll bring him in for questioning today
And then we'll see what Joseph has to say."

They said to Joe, "We know you took that ring."
But he replied, "I ain't done anything."
And swore to them upon the Trinity
That he'd not been in the vicinity,
But spent the whole day with his family,
And took them on an outing to the sea.

But they were sure he was the man they sought,
And very soon Joseph appeared in Court.
A youthful barrister, just qualified,
Defended the accused when he was tried.

He said his client had some days before
Been near the shop and may have touched the door
And left his fingerprint where it was found;
But certainly had never been around
Upon the day the ring had left the store
As he and family were by the shore
At Brighton, only for a single day,
As they could not afford a holiday.
The barrister played on this theme a lot,
And claimed Joe was a victim of a plot;
A poor man wrongly harried by police,
And only wanted to be left in peace.
He argued with a most impassioned plea
That Joe be released to his family.
A woman Juror then broke down and cried,
Thinking of Joe perhaps locked up inside.
Then spoke the Jury Foreman, deep and gruff,
And said, "My Lord, I think we've heard enough.
To carry on this trial there is no need;
A verdict of 'Not Guilty' we've agreed."
The Judge, surprised, could not believe his ears
As in his mind he'd given Joe two years.
The Jury's verdict surprised Joe still more;
With all the brushes he had with the Law
It was the first time he had been acquitted;
(He was, I have to say, somewhat dim-witted)
Thanking the barrister for everything,
He said, "Does that mean I can keep the ring?"

The host said, "That's a most amusing case.
I should have liked to see the Lawyer's face
When Joseph told him that he'd got the ring.

Now I must see what judgement I can bring.
Will it be you or yet another teller
Who'll claim the cask from Tabard's cellar.
As I've enjoyed each tale it's hard to choose,
So after dinner I will seek your views,
And if consensus is too hard a task
Then all will clearly have to share the cask.

But then upspoke a pilgrim in the crowd,
And said, "I'll tell a story if allowed.
I do not seek a prize or even glory,
But that I'm given leave to tell my story."
"Your story," said the host. "We'd like to hear.
We've time enough for that so never fear."

The Pilgrim's Tale

The strange events that I'm about to tell
Occurred some time ago in Israel.
A couple who had travelled far one day
Were looking for a place where they could stay.
As darkness fell an inn came into sight.
They asked if they could stay there for the night.
The host replied, "We have no rooms to spare,
And you will find it's just the same elsewhere.
The census has brought many folk to stay,
And some, like you have travelled a long way."
The girl said, "Have you nothing that is free?
I'm expecting soon as you can, no doubt, see."
The keeper of the inn saw her condition,
And said to her, "I have a proposition.
I'll put you up tonight if you are able
To put your beds inside my lowly stable."
The couple both agreed and that was done,
And to the girl that night was born a son.
There was no cushioned cot to lay his head;
A hay-filled manger had to do instead.
Shepherds in nearby fields were not asleep,
Instead were keeping watch for straying sheep.
When suddenly an angel did appear,
And startled them, but said, "You need not fear.
I've come to bring a message from on high.
It is to say that in the town nearby
Was born this night, within a stable bare,
The Saviour of the world." so, hurrying there,
They worshipped the young baby as he lay
In peaceful sleep upon the manger's hay.
When he was taken home the baby grew
Into a youth and man, and daily through

The passing years his wisdom did increase;
He never sinned but spoke of love and peace.
He left the fam'ly home aged thirty, and
With chosen few he travelled through the land
Preaching God's love to all, and by his might
Curing the sick and giving blind their sight.
He healed the lame and some from dead He raised,
And those who saw these wonders were amazed
At all the marv'lous things that He had done
And many said this surely is God's Son.
But he did also speak against the way
At which religious leaders of the day

Put their interpretation on the law
Resulting in oppression of the poor.
So they, fearing for their reputations,
Conspired and brought false accusations.
And though, sinless and innocent was He,
They had Him killed by nailing to a tree.
A cruel death for such a sinless one,
And they believed his influence was done.
But He arose, triumphant o'er the grave,
And lives today in Heaven, our souls to save
If we believe, and to His will consent
As did Archbishop Thomas down in Kent.
My friends this is the greatest story,
But telling it was not for my own glory;
So I don't want a prize, and so suggest
That you divide the ale among the rest.

So ends my tale of pilgrims as they went
With others on their way to Canterbury, Kent.
I hope that you've enjoyed the time
Spent reading this, my rather lengthy, rhyme.

Section VI

Christmastide Tales

Santa's Brainwave

It was the day before Christmas Eve, and Santa's reindeers were resting in preparation for their annual journey the next night. Blitzen nudged Prancer "Did you hear the weather forecast?" he asked. "Yes," replied Prancer, "it looks as if we are in for a fog that's going to last over Christmas."

"You know what that means," said Blitzen. "Santa will choose Rudolph to lead the team again, and he will boast about it for months."

"I know," said Prancer, "he was really insufferable the last time, but I can't see that there is much we can do about it."

"I don't know," said Dasher, who had been listening, "I have an idea." So that night, when all the other reindeers were asleep, Dasher went into Santa's workshop, where the elves were putting the finishing touches to some of the presents, and borrowed a tin of black enamel. He then went back to the reindeers' sleeping quarters and, carefully, so as not to awaken the sleeping Rudolph, he painted it over the latter's red nose.

The following night, just as forecast, there was a thick fog, and when Santa went out to harness the reindeer he put Rudolph in the lead just as Blitzen had predicted. But when they went out into the fog they could not see more than a yard ahead. "What's the matter, Rudolph?" shouted Santa.

"Why aren't you showing us the way?"

"I don't know," replied Rudolph, "there seems to be something the matter with my nose. It doesn't seem to be working."

"We'll never get round to all the houses at this rate," grumbled Santa, and then he had a brilliant idea. He reached into one of his sacks and pulled out a present which he quickly unwrapped to reveal a brand new satellite navigation receiver. "We'll use this," he said. Which is what they did, and they managed to deliver all the presents except one because, of course, they needed the Satnav receiver to find their way back home. So, if you did not get the Satnav receiver that you were expecting at Christmas you know who to blame!

Rudolph's Revenge

Rudolph was sulking. Now Santa had acquired his new satellite navigation receiver he did not need Rudolph to guide him on foggy nights and Rudolph felt aggrieved. "It's unfair!" He complained to Dasher, Donner and Blitzen who themselves had been replaced on Santa's team by three younger up-and-coming reindeer. "We've given the best years of our lives helping Santa deliver presents, and now we've been discarded like an unwanted pair of snow shoes."

"We could go on strike," said Dasher. Rudolph gave him a pitying look. "What good would that do?" said Rudolph, "as we're not wanted, nobody would notice. I've got a better idea. We know the route Santa takes. We can take the spare sleigh and follow him around and mix up all the presents he's left. Then people will complain that Santa and his new crew are not doing the job properly, and maybe we'll be reinstated. And this is what they decided, so if you find on Christmas Day you've been given a hand-knitted pink and green sweater two sizes too small, and junior unwraps a volume entitled 'Uplifting Victorian Verses' when he had asked for a Harry Potter book you will know the reason why.

Santa's Visitor

It was a few days before Christmas, and Santa had already been busy loading his sleigh in readiness for his annual round-the world delivery service, when he decided to take a short break. Then, from his armchair he noticed a stranger with a clip-board and briefcase standing by the front door.

"Good evening," said the stranger. "I am from the Ministry of Trade and Environment and we have been led to believe that you are proposing to take a load of goods out of the country without having the appropriate export licence in contravention of Section XVIII of the recent Carrier of Goods Act, and I am enforced to impound your sleigh and the goods therein until the aforesaid licence has been obtained. I shall leave you the necessary application form which you should forward to the Ministry where it will be carefully checked, and if it is in order you may expect to receive a licence within two to three months.

"But that's no good," said Santa. "People are expecting delivery on Christmas Eve."

"I am afraid that is impossible," said the stranger. "Which brings me to another point. We believe that you were proposing to use a number of animals, namely reindeer, to transport your sleigh to several foreign countries without the necessary certificates of health. Is that correct?"

"I've never heard such nonsense," replied Santa. "We've done this journey hundreds of times, and no-one has asked for a certificate of health before."

"Then I am afraid that this is really more serious than we thought," said the stranger, "because of the likelihood of Reindeer Flu and other diseases being introduced into this country and affecting indigenous cattle. So I have no alternative but to impound your herd immediately and check for infection and, if necessary, put the animals down. But don't worry. It will all be done very humanely." He then went out, leaving Santa dumbfounded in his armchair. Then he heard a loud bang, and was about to say "Oh, my poor reindeer," when he realised it was a bang on his front door, and that he had been asleep and dreaming.

He went to the door, and there stood a man with a briefcase in his hand who said, "Excuse me. I am from the Ministry of Trade and…"

If you don't get any presents this Christmas it is because Santa is awaiting trial on a charge of making a violent an unprovoked attack on a public servant who, it transpired, had merely come to ask if he could bring a party of children to see Santa's workshop!

Section VII

Inthe High Court of Justice Chance Division – before Mr Justice Undunne

Sykes v Brown
Judgement

Mr Justice Undunne

The facts of the case are quite straightforward. The defendant B owns a house having a rear garden which backs onto a public park. Between the garden and the park is a six-foot high wooden fence, on the garden side of which there is a bed of blackberry canes, the bed extending some four feet or so from the fence.

On the 30 April last, at approximately 3 am, the Defendant heard cries coming from the garden, and on investigation, he found the Plaintiff caught fast by the brambles and unable to extricate himself. The Defendant telephoned the Police Station, and two policemen eventually arrived in a patrol car. They took stock of the situation and, unable to help the Plaintiff because of strict health and safety regulations, called for the fire brigade and the ambulance services. Firemen released the Plaintiff and as he was found to have severe lacerations to his legs, hands and arms, he was transported by ambulance to the local hospital for treatment. He was subsequently discharged, but the wounds in his legs later became infected and he went as an in-patient to a private hospital for treatment, where he stayed for two weeks. He then took himself to a hotel on the South Coast for a period of convalescence.

He is now suing the Defendant for damages for the following:-

(a) Post-traumatic stress due to suffering while trapped by the brambles.
(b) The loss of clothes damaged by the brambles
(c) The cost of his stay at the private hospital and subsequently at the hotel while recuperating.
(d) The loss of earnings while incapacitated.

The Defendant has contested all of the Plaintiffs claims, arguing that the Plaintiff had no right to be in the garden, which he must have entered for some illegal and nefarious purposes. This, he said, was borne out by the subsequent finding of a housebreaking implement, commonly known as a jemmy, amongst the brambles, not far from where the Plaintiff was trapped.

However the Defendant has not produced any evidence of a link between the implement and the Plaintiff, so there is nothing to support his allegation, and I have no option but to disregard it.

On the other hand, the Plaintiff has given a logical explanation of the reason that he was in the garden at the time in question. He claimed that his nephew or grandson (he did not appear to be sure which – but this is perfectly understandable after the terrifying ordeal he has gone through) had accidentally lost a ball over the Defendant's fence the previous day while playing in the park, and he had offered to retrieve it. However he was not able to do so during daylight hours as he had other business to attend to, and it was about twelve o'clock at night that he remembered his promise and, so as not to disappoint the child, he decided to retrieve the ball then.

When asked, under cross-examination, why he didn't go to the front door, the Plaintiff replied that he was reluctant to disturb the household at such an hour for something so trivial as a lost ball. A very commendable attitude I must say.

When asked why he had placed blackberry canes at a position close to the fence, the Defendant replied that he was very partial to blackberries. However there are other equally delicious fruits that he could have planted which would have been no danger to members of the public seeking to recover lost property. Strawberry plants spring to mind, and I am told that strawberries are a most sought-after delicacy in the district of Wimbledon at a certain time of the year. I cannot, therefore, accept the Defendant's explanation that he planted blackberry canes where he did. He reluctantly admitted, under cross-examination, that they were placed there 'as a deterrent'. However to be a deterrent the person to whom it is addressed must be given some prior warning of the danger. In the Defendant's case this could be, for example, the attachment to the outside of the fence a notice reading 'Beware of the Blackberries' in a manner in which some householders put a notice on their front gate warning callers of the presence of a dog.

However no such notice was given, and the first the Plaintiff knew of the blackberries was when he was caught fast by his legs.

I can only conclude, therefore, that the blackberry canes were deliberately planted there for the purpose of unlawfully and maliciously trapping unwary members of the public endeavouring to recover their lost property. I am therefore of the opinion that the Defendant was clearly responsible for the injuries and damage and consequent trauma suffered by the Plaintiff.

The use of spring-loaded mechanical man traps which operate to grip the leg of a person unwary enough to tread on them has long been illegal, and I can see no difference between a mechanical man trap and a herbaceous equivalent. At the completion of this case, therefore, I will forward the papers to the Director of Public Prosecutions.

Turning now to the matter of compensation – the Plaintiff has undoubtedly suffered an alarming and painful experience, trapped, as he was, for some hours with serious injuries to his legs and arms, and I do not find the claim of two hundred thousand pounds for the suffering and trauma excessive in the circumstances. The Defendant has queried the claimed cost of a new suit to replace the one damaged by the brambles, disputing the need to purchase a made-to-measure one from a leading designer. However the Plaintiff has said that he would not feel comfortable in an off-the-peg suit from one of the national high-street stores, which I find perfectly understandable. Similarly the Defendant has objected to the Plaintiff using a private hospital to cure his infected leg, but the Plaintiff has said that he needed rest and quiet in order to recuperate which he could not have obtained in a public ward. This again is perfectly understandable, as is the choice of the five star Grand Hotel for his convalescence.

I now come to the claim for loss of earnings, which the Plaintiff has said to amount to three thousand a week 'on a good day' whatever that may mean. But he has not provided any evidence of the amount of such loss such as a statement from the income tax authorities. Reluctantly, therefore, I have no alternative but to reject that claim. However the Plaintiff has succeeded in the remainder of the claims and I hold that the Defendant must pay the costs of the proceedings.

The Defendant has counterclaimed for damage to the blackberries, but such damage was not caused by the Plaintiff; quite the reverse in fact. The damage was caused by the firemen who released him. The Defendant is quite at liberty to take action against the fire brigade, should he so wish.

Mrs X v SMITH

Judgement

Mr Justice Undunne

This case has arisen from an incident that took place on the 4th July last year. Mrs X is taking action against the Defendant, Smith, on behalf of her son Master X who cannot be named for legal reasons.

The facts of the case are straightforward and not in dispute as there were a number of witnesses present when the incident took place.

Mrs P, a senior citizen, had just emerged from her local Post Office after drawing her retirement pension and saw a boy, now known as Master X, running off with her handbag in which she had placed her pension money. Mrs P called out 'Stop Thief', a slanderous accusation as it now turns out, whereupon Mr Smith, himself a pensioner and an ex-footballer, tripped Master X up from behind and sat on him until the police arrived some fifteen minutes later, having been alerted by Mr Smith on his mobile telephone. In the meantime Mrs P had caught up with them and, after retrieving her handbag, used it to belabour Master X about the head. I understand that, as a result of her action, Mrs P was charged with child abuse and criminal assault, but because of extenuating circumstances, her age and her previous exemplary record, she was merely placed on probation and bound over to keep the peace.

Mrs X, on behalf of her son, is suing Mr Smith for injuries caused to her son by Mr Smith's action, irreparable damage to Master X's designer clothing and trainers, and severe traumatic stress as a result of his distressing experience. As a single parent on supplementary benefit she is entitled to legal aid, and Mr Pennypinch QC is acting on her behalf.

Mr Smith, who I understand is at the moment in one of Her Majesty's prisons awaiting trial on charges of child abuse, grievous bodily harm, criminal damage and illegal restraint of a minor as a result of the incident in question, is defending the action himself.

In response to Mr Pennypinch's questioning Master X explained that on the day of the incident, he was hurrying to get to school and did not realise his arm had caught Mrs P's handbag until she came up after he had been tripped up and took it from him. If he had realised before, he would naturally have gone back and returned it to her.

On cross-examination by Mr Smith, Master X admitted that he had not been to school for some two or three weeks prior to the incident, but he explained that this was because he was always being picked on by the teachers as, due to the time spent in helping his mother at home, he was frequently late and rarely had time to do any homework. He was accordingly hurrying on that day to get to school as he did not want to get into any further trouble, and that is why he did not notice he had caught his arm in Mrs P's handbag.

Mrs X, in giving evidence, said that Master X was a very kind and loving son, and quite often brought her presents and small gifts of money which he said he had obtained by doing odd jobs, and therefore couldn't imagine he had intended to take Mrs P's handbag as Mr Smith has alleged. She added that since the incident her son had become very withdrawn and had a psychological fear of going to school in case he was attacked again.

On cross-examination, Mrs X, when asked how it was that, as she was on supplementary benefit, she was able to purchase designer clothing for her son. She replied that Master X bought these articles himself as she had to spend what money she had looking after them both and he did not want her to be burdened with the additional costs involved in buying expensive clothing for him. A very commendable attitude I must say.

Under cross-examination, Mr Smith admitted that on one occasion, when playing a game of football, he was sent off the field by the referee as a result of rashly handling the ball in his own penalty area to prevent a goal being scored, which I understand is against the rules of the game. It appears that he is still prone to act precipitately and recklessly without due prior consideration, and has now admitted that he was unwise to act as he did on the day in question. One cannot fully emphasize that the public should not take matters into their own hands on such an occasion. The correct action that should have been taken by Mr Smith on hearing Mrs P call out would have been to ask her what the matter was and then alert the police on his mobile who would then have arrived to take down details of what had occurred so that they could then have taken any action they deemed appropriate.

Accordingly I find for Mrs and Master X on all counts, and the question now arises on the amount of damages I should award. As regards personal injuries to Master X, I see from the hospital report that these were only of a minor nature which did not involve a stay in hospital, and the only costs involved were the fares of taxis to and from the hospital amounting to twenty-five pounds, so I award this sum in respect of Master X's injuries. Turning now to the cost of the damaged designer clothing, neither Mrs nor Master X has produced any receipts for the clothing, but I understand that articles of this kind are somewhat expensive and are much sought after by the younger generation. Mrs X has asked for one thousand and five hundred pounds, but as I am able to purchase a very commendable suit with a shirt, together with a stylish pair of shoes for around one thousand pounds, I am of the opinion that the sum asked for is rather more than is warranted and consider an award of eleven hundred pounds is quite sufficient in respect of such damage. As to the question of traumatic stress, I understand that such a problem can be very serious and may have repercussions in later life, but Master X is quite young and his demeanour in the witness box was such that I do not consider that he is likely to be troubled by serious after-effects, so I believe an award of damages of twenty thousand pounds would be adequate in the circumstances. If this sum is considered inadequate, Mrs X, on behalf of Master X, is perfectly eligible to appeal. They are also awarded the costs in this case.

Section VIII

Remembrances

A Waaf Remembers

I shivered at the sight of what had been
an active airfield in my younger days,
Where men, no more than boys, were to be seen boarding
their planes at dusk where sheep now graze.
I still recall that ev'ning long ago when a young sergeant
caught my passing glance.
He came towards me bashfully and slow and shyly asked me
if I cared to dance.
I did, and then in the ensuing days
We grew to know each other better, and
Love blossomed fiercer than a wind-fuelled blaze.
Long did we talk, our life together planned.
Then one black night, above the Ruhr, his plane was lost. I
never saw my love again.

Regrets

There were so many things, I know,
I could have done, my love to show;
A close embrace, a gentle touch,
A passing kiss could mean so much;
A soft caressing of your hair;
My cheek on yours to show I care,
And 'Love you' whispered in your ear.
Alas you can no longer hear,
As you, my darling have passed on
And opportunities have gone.

A Veteran's Farewell

When I am gone away, do not shed tears,
For I've long passed mankind's allotted years,
And in my time I've countless marvels seen
Which were undreamt of long ago, and been
Privileged to travel far and wide, and
View world famous places at first hand.
I've had the love of wife and family,
And many friends who have supported me.
Throughout my life I have been surely blest;
I've no regrets as I go to my rest;
For I've faced death before, but was spared then,
When many that I knew, much better men,
Were lost; I've lived on borrowed time for years.
I've had my life; of going I've no fears.
So then I'll have to bid you all adieu,
But do not grieve; you've better things to do.
For death will come to all of us in time;
Just think of me as I was in my prime.

Obituaries

If you should read of my demise
Do not let teardrops cloud your eyes.
Just say, relieved, wheree're you be
"I'm jolly glad it isn't me."

Please Take Your Seat
(A One-Act Play)

CAST
Charles Robinson MP; Margaret, his wife.
Jenny, an old friend of Charles.
Liz, a young reporter.
Charlie Bagshaw MP, Minister of Local Affairs.
Polly, Charlie's Secretary.
Roger.

The action takes place in the living room of Charles Robinson's constituency cottage. A kitchen opens off the living room at one side of the stage, and stairs lead up to bedrooms at the opposite side of the stage. The front door opens directly into the living room.

SCENE I

One morning shortly before a general election,

Charles   (to himself, sorting the post) junk mail, begging letter, junk mail, begging letter…

Margaret   (from the kitchen) Was that the post?

Charles: Yes, (to himself) begging letter, begging letter. Hello, what's this?

Margaret   (entering room) Anything for me?

Charles: I don't think so.

Margaret: Why are you smelling that pink envelope?

Charles   Err, just checking for explosives

Margaret   I thought there were dogs for doing that

Charles: (hesitatingly) Well, they're not always available, so we have to take precautions

Margaret: I wouldn't have thought there could be enough explosive in that small envelope to blow out a candle. Why don't you open it?
(Charles does so)

Margaret: Well. Who is it from?

Charles   It's er from an old constituent.

Margaret   Probably wanting you to press for increased old age pensions. That wouldn't be a bad idea. We might need one ourselves one day. Have you any bigwigs coming to support you at the election meeting tonight?

Charles   Yes. The Minister of Local Affairs.

Margaret: Oh, not Charlie Bagshaw. You would have thought that they could have sent someone like the Foreign Secretary or the Chancellor

Charles: The bigshots will be going to the marginal seats

Margaret: If Charlie gets going, this will probably become a marginal seat. Whatever you do don't let him say anything about the proposed

	bypass. You know that half the constituents are for it and the other half against, so whatever he says is likely to upset half your voters
Charles:	He's not due to say anything about it, but if he's asked, he'll probably say something like 'We'll carry out a detailed survey after consultation with all the interested parties, and carefully consider all the views put forward so we can come to a conclusion satisfactory to all concerned'.
Margaret	How can it be satisfactory to all concerned when half are for it and the other half against?
Charles	Well as there's not likely to be a decision until after the election it won't matter.
Margaret	But suppose someone asks him what his views are?
Charles	Oh, the Chairman's an old hand at that sort of thing. He'll say 'I think we've covered this subject. Next question please' and point to someone in our party who he knows has a pre-arranged quite innocuous question.
Margaret	I hope you know best. I expect he'll want to stay here and bring his latest floosie with hi
Charles:	You mean his private secretary
Margaret:	Whatever she calls herself. Why can't they stay at a hotel?
Charles:	I expect he prefers home comforts
Margaret	And claim hotel expenses I expect. Are you sure you don't mind me going to my sister's instead of going to tonight's election meeting? She didn't sound at all well on the phone, and particularly wanted me to come.
Charles:	No, that's all right if she really needs you. But what about her husband?
Margaret:	Oh, Tom's useless in an emergency. He's a man

Charles	I should hope so. But you never can tell these days
Margaret	Anyway I must fly. I've ordered a taxi to take me to the station, and that sounds like it now. I'll probably only be away overnight. Goodbye (kiss)
	(Margaret leaves through front door)
Charles	(reading) "Dear Charles, I know it's been a long time since we parted, but I wonder if I, for old times' sake, you would do something for me. After all we were very friendly once. I'll explain everything when I see you. All my love Jenny."
	(to himself) Dear Jenny, I wonder what she wants after all these years. (A knock on door) Come in, it's not locked.
Jenny	Hello Charles. Aren't you glad to see me?
Charles	Jenny! I wasn't expecting you so soon. I've only just received your letter. What is it all about?
Jenny	I just came on the off chance to see you. It was all rather difficult to explain by letter. Was that your wife who has just gone out
Charles	Yes. She's gone to see her sister in London.
Jenny	Good. Now we can have a good long talk. Do you remember the first time we went away together to Brighton?
Charles	Yes. The owner of that small hotel looked at us rather suspiciously when we booked in, especially at your grandmother's old wedding ring
Jenny	Well you shouldn't have signed the book Mr and Mrs Smith.
Charles	It was the only name I could think of on the spur of the moment. Anyway she changed completely the following day and couldn't do enough for us. Why do you think that was?

135

Jenny	Didn't you know? I dropped a little confetti I'd saved from my cousin's wedding in our bedroom the first night we were there and she thought we really were on our honeymoon. I also explained about my grandmother's wedding ring. I told her that my widowed mother couldn't pay for the wedding, so you had to, and as a result you couldn't afford to pay for a new ring. She was all over you then and I noticed that she gave you extra helpings at mealtimes.
Charles	But that wasn't true. Both your parents were alive and well off
Jenny	Yes but she didn't know that
Charles	I never knew what a schemer you were. Anyway you wanted me to help you in some way. What is it?
Jenny:	Well, didn't you wonder why I left you and disappeared?
Charles	Yes, of course. I was very upset. You didn't even write.
Jenny	I'm really very sorry, and it's very difficult to tell you, but we've got a son.
Charles	What. You mean you and me?
Jenny	Well, there's no-one else here is there?
Charles:	Why didn't you tell me at the time?
Jenny	Well, I knew you wanted to go into politics, and I thought that if it got out it would spoil your chances of being selected. You know what it was like in those days.
	It's been very difficult bringing our son up on my own, but I've never asked you for anything before, and I was wondering if you could let me have ten thousand pounds to help him go to university?
Charles	I can see you must have had a very hard time and I'm willing to be able to help.

136

	Would a cheque do?
Jenny	Yes please. You're a darling. Make it out to bearer as I don't want you to know our son's name
Charles	(writing a cheque) Here you are. I'm only too glad to help. But you must admit it has been rather a shock. Does he know who I am?
Jenny	Of course not darling. I couldn't tell him you were an MP, could I? I told him that you were a property developer. Now don't look like that, darling. Some property developers are quite respectable.
Charles	And MPs aren't, I suppose
Jenny	You know I didn't mean it like that. I thought there would be less chance of him finding out who you were and making life difficult for you now that you are married. Now, as it's been such a shock to you, make yourself comfortable and I'll go and make you a cup of coffee. I know just how you like it. The kitchen's through here I imagine
Charles:	Yes. Thank you.
	(Jenny goes into kitchen)
Charles	(to himself). A son eh? After all these years. I wonder if he looks like me.
Jenny	shrieks from the kitchen) Whoever left that spoon in the sink? (Comes into the living room) Just look at me. My dress is all wet down the front. I'll have to take it off and dry it (commences to do so).
Charles	No, not here. Our bedroom is at the top of the stairs. In the wardrobe you'll find my wife's dresses. Put one of those on while your own dries. You're more or less the same size
Jenny:	All right (goes upstairs).

Charles	(to himself) Fancy that. A son (a knock on the door) Come in, it's not locked. (Enter Liz)
Liz	Thank you
Charles:	Are you a constituent. No you can't be you're not old enough.
Liz	Everybody says that. I have to show proof of my age when I want to buy a drink, and it's not fair because my friend is younger than me but looks older and she doesn't have to. I'm nineteen, you know.
Charles:	Anyway who are you and what is it you wanted?
Liz	I'm the new political reporter from the local Weekly Gazette, and I'd like to interview you
Charles	Why? What's happened to Barry?
Liz	He's been promoted. He now does the sports pages. ?
Charles	Is that a promotion
Liz	Of course it is. More people read the sports pages than the political columns Anyway I want to make the political column more personal. A lot of readers would be interested to know about your personal life that's why I've come to see you.
Jenny:	(from stairs holding a dress) Will this one do darling?
Charles	(to Liz) Have you met my wife?
Liz	No, I've never had the opportunity
Charles	Good (to Jenny) Yes darling, that will do nicely. This is Liz. She's a reporter. A REPORTER. (to Liz) She wants to know if that dress will be suitable for the meeting tonight. (to Jenny) Why don't you go and put

it on? I'm sure Liz didn't want to see you in
your underclothes.

(Jenny disappears into bedroom)

Liz   Oh, I don't mind. I hope to do the fashion page
             one day.

Charles   : Is that a promotion?
Liz   Of course. More people look at it than the
             political column. The women look at the
             fashions and the men look at the models
Charles: Of course. How silly of me. But you' ll have
             to excuse me now as I've got a lot to do
             before the meeting tonight. We'll have our
             talk later.
Liz   Yes, of course
Charles   Good, I'll see you later
Liz   Thank you. Good bye. (goes out of front
             door).
Jenny   Yes, but that's torn it. She thinks you're my
             wife. You'd better go to the meeting tonight so
             that she can see you there, but you needn't
             stay. Make some excuse. Say you've got a
             headache or something and you have to leave
             early. You can come back here and stay the
             night if you like

Jenny   I'd love to come. Just like old times darling,
             but I won't hold you up now. I'll go back to
             my hotel and see you later.

             (Curtain – end of Scene I)

139

SCENE II

(Clock strikes six o'clock – a knock on the door – Charles opens it)

Charles	Oh, hello Charlie, I've been expecting you
Charlie	Thank you, it's nice to see you. This is Pauline known as Polly. Is it all right to stay here?
Charles	Yes, of course. I'm afraid Margaret isn't here. Some family trouble. She's gone to her sister's for the night but I don't think it's anything serious
Charlie	Well give her my regards. I'll just go and get our stuff from the car. (Goes out)
Charles	Nice to meet you Polly. So you're Charlie's new secretary?
Polly	Yes but I prefer to call him Charles. It's more refined, don't you think? There was a king called Charles you know, but he lost his head
Charles	Yes I did know. Two kings actually
Polly	Did they both lose their heads?
Charles	Yes, one literally and the other one figuratively over an actress called Nell Gwynne. Will you be coming to the meeting this evening?
Polly:	No, it's too boring. All they do is talk. I'll probably have an early night. (Charlie enters).
Charlie	Here's our luggage. Can you tell us where to put it?
Charles	Yes OK. I'll show you. It's upstairs on the left.
	(They all go upstairs) (End of Scene II)

140

SCENE III

Margaret:	You can come in Roger. Charles will still be at his meeting. It's only just gone nine o'clock. I'm sorry I couldn't go on with it
Roger:	You seemed so keen at first. Why did you change your mind?
Margaret:	Yes I know I was. It was because Charles was always busy with committees and meetings, and didn't seem to have much time for me. I was just looking for a bit of excitement when I met you, but in the end I decided that I couldn't be unfaithful to him. I really am sorry are you very disappointed?
Roger	Terribly
Margaret	You sound just like Noel Coward. I must go and freshen up. There's the kitchen Make yourself a cup of coffee or have something stronger if you would like. You'll find the bottles in the left hand cupboard. I won't be a moment.
Roger	Right
	(Margaret goes upstairs and Roger goes into the kitchen) (Jenny enters through front door)
Jenny	to herself) Thank goodness that's over. I couldn't get away from Liz. She kept asking me what it was like to be an MP's wife. I just hope I gave her all the right answers.

141

	(Jenny goes towards kitchen as Roger comes out)
Jenny and Roger	(together) What on earth are you doing here?
Jenny	You first
Roger	It was like this. I planned to take Robinson's wife to a hotel for the night, take some photographs of her in bed, and see if she would be prepared to pay some money to prevent me from sending them to her husband
Jenny	But that's immoral. When we started this game we agreed only to target those celebrities that were being genuinely having affairs, and not start anything ourselves.
Roger	I know, but times are getting hard. These days many victims targeted won't pay up like they used to. They just laugh because they enjoy the publicity, so I thought I would branch out despite what we originally agreed
Jenny	I still think it's immoral, but why are you here?
Roge	She chickened out at the last moment, so I brought her home. But what about you? I hope you weren't going to do the same with her husband
Jenny:	No, I thought I might get him to give me ten thousand pounds to help pay for our son to go to university
Roger	We haven't got a son
Jenny	I meant his and mine
Roger	You didn't tell me you had a son
Jenny	I haven't. It's just what I told him to get the money

Roger	That sounds like blackmail
Jenny	No it isn't. He was quite happy to pay me out of the goodness of his heart.
Roger:	I didn't know MPs had a heart. Has he given you any money then?
Jenny	Yes. He's really quite sweet. He gave me a cheque.
Roger	In that case I think it advisable if we just disappear before he comes back from his meeting. I've got the car outside. I don't know what's happened to Margaret. She went upstairs to freshen up she said, and she might come down any minute.
Jenny	Yes. We'd better get off. Just stop at the hotel so I can pick up my things, and you can take me to the hotel where you were going to take Margaret. As you've booked a room we might as well stay the night
Roger	Right. Let's go
	(Jenny and Roger exit through front door)
Margaret	(coming downstairs) Roger, Roger, I think I may have dozed off. You'd better be going. Charles will be home shortly. (To herself) Oh, he seems to have gone already. That's just as well. Otherwise I would have had some explaining to do.
	(Charles enters)
Charles	I'm back. Oh, Margaret, it's you
Margaret:	Who did you think it was?

Charles	It's rather unexpected. I didn't expect you back until tomorrow. How's your sister?
Margaret:	Oh, much better, thank you. That's why I decided to come home. Aren't you glad to see me?
Charles	Yes, of course I am. (They kiss)
Margaret	Did Charlie come?
Charles	Yes, he'll be along shortly. He's met someone he knows
Polly	(from upstairs) Is that you Charles? Aren't you coming to bed?
Margaret	Brute. Philanderer (Margaret slaps Charles's face) I'm just away for a night and you bring a woman in. After all these years we've been married,
Charles	That hurt. It's not me, but it's Charlie she wants.
Margaret:	: But she said Charles
Charles:	Yes, I know. But she calls Charlie that.She says it's more refined. (Enters Charlie)
Charlie	Hello. Am I interrupting something? (to Margaret) It's nice to see you Margaret. Charles said you'd be away for the night.
Margaret:	Yes, I had to come back suddenly
Charles	Everything's OK; thank you, but you'd better go and see Polly She wants to know when you're going to bed. Margaret thought it was me she wanted
Charlie	That's a laugh. No accounting for tastes. I'd better go up then. Good night. See you in the morning. (Goes upstairs)

Margaret	I'm so sorry darling, but what was I to think when she said Charles?
Charles	You ought to know me better than that. Suppose I were to accuse you of going out with another man. It's just ridiculous
Margaret	Yes, I've said I'm sorry.
	(A knock on the door. Charles opens it. Liz enters)
Liz	Oh, Mr Robinson. I'm sorry to interrupt, but just wanted to come and tell you that I thought your speech tonight was terrific.
Margaret	: Charles, won't you introduce us?
Charles:	Er, er yes. This is Liz. A political reporter for the local paper.
Liz:	And who are you?
Margaret	I'm Mr Robinson's wife
Liz:	His wife? Oh (penny drops) OH. If you'll excuse me. I must fly. I've a deadline to meet
	(Liz exits)
	(Curtain – end of Scene III)

SCENE IV

(The following morning. The front door is open and Charles and Margaret are waving their visitors good-bye)

Margaret   Thank goodness they've gone. I can't see what Charlie sees in her, or what she sees in him come to that. You've been looking serious since that Liz went off so suddenly last night. I wonder why she did.

Charles: I've been thinking about that. I'll probably ring the Gazette's Chief Editor later, and find out what he has to say

Margaret   All right, you do that. I want to pop out and get a few things from the shops, but I won't be long.

     (Margaret puts on a coat and exits through front door

Charles: speaking on telephone) Is that The Gazette? This is Charles Robinson MP, could you please put me through to the Chief Editor.
     (pause)
     Is that you Peter? This is Charles. You know that you were interested in buying the paddock at the bottom of our garden. Well I've changed my mind and I'm quite prepared to let you have it if you're still interested.
     (pause)
     You are? Good. I was thinking of twelve thousand pounds.
     (pause)
     Oh. I see. Well as we are old friends, I am quite prepared to do you a favour and make it ten thousand.
     (pause)

Oh, good. In return, could you do me a favour? It's about your new political columnist. I saw her last night and there seems to have been a bit of a mix-up and she appears to have got hold of the wrong end of a stick. So, I should be grateful if you wouldn't print anything she might have said about last night.

(pause)

Yes, I know it's awkward, and she won't like it, but can't you tell her it's a matter of national importance or you're short of space or something. I'm sure you can think of a good reason. I'm sure that you wouldn't want to get involved in a messy libel action. I tell you what. Yesterday evening she let slip that she would like to work on the fashion page. Could you suggest that you make her assistant editor of that page if she is prepared to forget everything that happened yesterday. I'm sure that she'll jump at it.

(pause)

Good thank you. In the meantime I'll get on to my lawyer about the paddock. (replaces phone) Phew, that's a relief.

(Margaret enters and the phone rings. She answers it)

Margaret	Yes, he's here. Who is it? (Hands phone to Charles) It's that girl Liz
Charles:	on phone) Yes, I thought you would be pleased. Good luck. (replaces phone
Margaret:	What did she want?
Charles:	She wanted to work on the fashion page so I put in a good word for her with the paper's editor
Margaret	Why did you do that?

147

Charles:	Well, I always like to help my constituents if I can. Perhaps she will vote for me at the election. Margaret dear, I think I've been neglecting you recently, with one thing and another. Would you like to go out to dinner this evening?
Margaret	That would be lovely.

(Curtain – end of Scene IV)